Charlie and the Chocolate Factory

Text copyright © 2008 Longtail Books
Charlie and the Chocolate Factory illustrations © 1995 Quentin Blake

이 책에 사용된 일러스트 사용 권한은 A P Watt Ltd를 통해 계약한 롱테일북스에 있습니다.
한국 내에서 보호받는 저작물이므로 무단 전재와 무단 복제를 금합니다.

원서 읽는 단어장
Charlie and the Chocolate Factory

1판 1쇄 2009년 2월 9일
1판 18쇄 2025년 6월 9일

기획 이수영
책임편집 김수진
콘텐츠 제작 Michael Allen Misner·롱테일 교육 연구소
마케팅 두잉글 사업본부

펴낸이 이수영
펴낸곳 롱테일북스
출판등록 제2015-000191호
주소 04033 서울특별시 마포구 양화로 113, 3층(서교동, 순흥빌딩)
전자메일 help@ltinc.net

ISBN 978-89-5605-320-2 14740
     978-89-5605-319-6 (세트)

Contents

원서 읽는 단어장 소개 · 4
이 책의 구성 · 6
영어 원서 읽기 전문가가 대답해주는 FAQ · · · · · · · · · · · · 10

Chapter 1-5
Comprehension Quiz · 14
Build Your Vocabulary · 24
Crossword Puzzle · 30

Chapter 9-10
Comprehension Quiz · 32
Build Your Vocabulary · 42
Crossword Puzzle · 50

Chapter 11-15
Comprehension Quiz · 52
Build Your Vocabulary · 60
Crossword Puzzle · 68

Chapter 16-20
Comprehension Quiz · 70
Build Your Vocabulary · 80
Crossword Puzzle · 90

Chapter 21-25
Comprehension Quiz · 92
Build Your Vocabulary · 102
Crossword Puzzle · 112

Chapter 26-30
Comprehension Quiz · 114
Build Your Vocabulary · 124
Crossword Puzzle · 132

Answers
Comprehension Quiz Answers · 136
Crossword Puzzle Answers · 138

원서 읽는 단어장 소개

누구나 추천하는 최고의 영어 공부법, 영어 원서 읽기!

최근 영어 원서 읽기가 영어 공부법으로 주목받고 있습니다. 영어를 많이 접하는 것이 영어 실력을 향상시키는 가장 바람직한 방법이라는 공감대가 형성되면서, 쉽고 저렴하게 영어를 접할 수 있는 '원서 읽기'가 그 대안으로 각광받고 있는 것이지요.

실제로도 영어 좀 한다는 사람들이 원서 읽기를 추천하거나 어린 아이들이 엄마표 영어 연수 등을 통해 원서를 읽는 많은 사례들을 인터넷 상에서 쉽게 찾아볼 수 있습니다.

원서 읽기를 위한 최고의 친구, 『원서 읽는 단어장』!!

원서가 좋은 영어 공부 수단이긴 하지만, 한 번쯤 원서를 읽어본 독자들은 대부분 다음과 같은 고민을 하곤 합니다.

누가 여기 나오는 단어 좀 찾아주면 안되나?
모르는 단어가 나올 때마다 사전을 찾을 수도 없고,
그렇다고 그냥 지나치자니 뭔가 찜찜한데...

지금 내가 제대로 읽고 이해하고 있는 걸까?
번역된 책을 찾아서 일일이 대조할 수도 없고,
뭔가 확인할 방법이 있었으면 좋겠는데...

이런 문제를 해결해주고자, 여기 『원서 읽는 단어장』이 왔습니다!
원서 읽는 단어장은, 영어 원서에 나온 어려운 어휘들을 완벽히 정리해서 원서 읽기의 부담감을 줄이고 보다 효과적으로 영어 실력을 쌓을 수 있도록 도와주는 책입니다. 또한 이해력을 점검하는 Comprehension Quiz를 통해 내가 원서를 정확히 읽고 있는지 확인해볼 수 있습니다.

『원서 읽는 단어장』시리즈를 통해 영어 원서를 보다 쉽고 재미있게 읽고, 영어 실력도 쑥쑥 향상시켜보세요.

이 책은 Roald Dahl(로알드 달)의 대표작 Charlie and the Chocolate Factory(찰리와 초콜릿 공장) 독자들을 위해 만들어졌습니다. 위 영어 원서는 시중 서점 및 인터넷 서점에서 쉽게 구입할 수 있습니다.

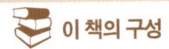 이 책의 구성

Comprehension Quiz

원서를 제대로 읽고 이해하고 있는지 측정해보는 간단한 퀴즈입니다.

원어민 Extensive Reading 전문가가 출제한 쉽고 재미있는 문제들로 구성되어 있습니다. 퀴즈를 풀어보고 틀린 부분이 있다면, 제대로 이해한 것이 맞는지 해당 내용을 다시 한 번 점검해봐야겠죠?

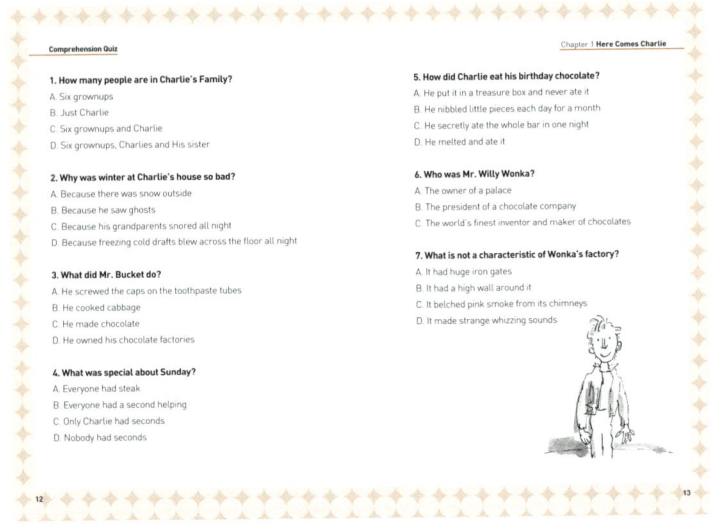

퀴즈는 각 챕터별로 약 5개 안팎의 문제가 출제되어 있습니다.

각 챕터를 읽고 바로 문제를 풀어보는 것도 좋고, 혹은 시간이 되는 대로 쭉 읽은 후 해당 부분만큼 문제를 풀어보는 것도 좋은 방법입니다. 내 상황과 스타일에 맞게 적절히 활용하세요!

정답은 136페이지에 있습니다.

Build your Vocabulary

원서에 등장하는 어려운 어휘가 정리되어 있습니다.

단어는 각 챕터별로, 원서에서 단어가 등장하는 순서 그대로 정리되어 있으며, [빈도-스펠링-발음기호-한글 뜻-영어 뜻] 순으로 표기되어 있습니다.

별표(★)가 많을수록 필수 어휘입니다. 또 이전 챕터에서 등장한 중요 어휘가 반복해서 나올 때는 '**복습**'이라고 표시해서 정리했습니다.

특히 로알드 달(Roald Dahl)의 대표 세 작품(Charlie and the Chocolate Factory, Matilda, James and the Giant Peach) 단어장에는 빈도 표시와 함께 **M**(Matilda에도 나오는 어휘) 또는 **J**(James and the Giant Peach에도 나오는 어휘) 표시가 되어 있습니다. 이런 단어를 확실히 암기해두면, 이후 시리즈를 읽을 때 큰 도움이 됩니다.

어휘 목록 중에 아주 기초적인 어휘는 제외되어 있습니다. 원서를 읽을 때 여기 나와 있는 단어 외에도 모르는 어휘가 너무 많다면, '내 영어 수준보다 지나치게 어려운 책을 골랐다'는 의미가 됩니다. 이런 경우에는 일단 더 쉬운 원서에 도전하는 것이 좋은 방법입니다.

여기 정리된 단어를 일일이 손으로 쓰면서 '암기'하려고 하지는 마세요! 실질적인 어휘 암기는 원서를 읽으면서 문맥 속에서 단어와 자주 마주칠 때 이루어집니다!
단어 리스트는 원서를 읽기 전, 후에 눈으로 쭉 살피면서 '단어와 익숙해지도록' 만드는 데 활용하세요. 원서를 읽을 때 단어에서 오는 부담감이 줄어들고, 매우 효율적으로 어휘 실력을 향상시킬 수 있습니다.

Crossword Puzzle

잠시 쉬어가면서 낱말 맞추기 퍼즐을 하는 페이지입니다.
각 문제에 해당하는 단어 스펠링을 가로-세로 빈칸에 맞춰서 채워나가면 됩니다.

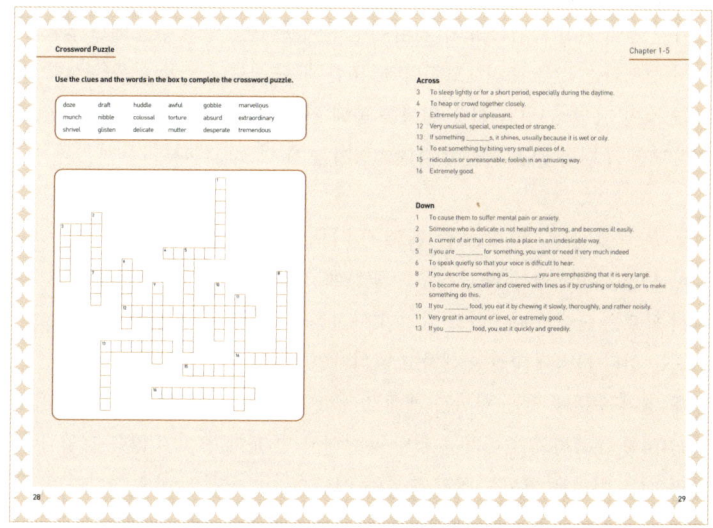

퍼즐의 문제들은 원서에서 반복해서 등장하는 중요 어휘로 구성되어 있습니다. 편안한 마음으로 퍼즐을 풀어보세요! 그러다보면 어휘 실력도 더욱 탄탄하게 다져질 것입니다.

정답은 138 페이지에 있습니다.

영어 원서 읽기 전문가가 대답해주는 FAQ

Q. 원서를 읽고 싶은데 어떤 책으로 시작할지 모르겠어요.

A. 원서를 고를 때는 '나의 영어 수준'과 '나의 관심 분야', 이 두 가지만 생각하면 됩니다. 꼭 읽고 싶은 책이 내 영어 수준에도 적합하다면, 그게 설사 영어로 쓰여 있다 해도 쉽고 재미있게 읽을 수 있습니다. 한글로 감명 깊게 읽었던 책이나 전공·업무에 연관된 책 중에서 수준에 맞는 원서를 찾아보세요. 베스트셀러 소설이나 자기 계발서 중에서 골라 읽는 것도 좋은 방법입니다.

아직 영어 원서 읽기 초보자라면, 관심 분야보다는 '영어 수준'에 초점을 맞춰서 선택하는 것을 추천해드립니다. 또한 내 수준보다 조금 쉬운 원서를 고르는 것이 더 좋습니다. 쉬운 원서를 통해 완독의 기쁨을 맛보고 4~5권 이상 읽다보면 그 다음 읽을 책들이 자연스럽게 눈에 띌 것입니다!

Q. 원서를 읽을 때 모르는 단어가 나오면 어떻게 하죠?

A. 사전을 찾으면서 읽는 경우는 중간에 지쳐 포기할 확률이 높습니다. 따라서 모르는 단어가 나온다고 일일이 사전을 찾으면서 읽지는 마세요. 모르는 어휘는 일단 문맥에 따라 이해하고 넘어가면 됩니다.

내 영어 수준에 맞는 원서를 제대로 골랐다면, 어려운 어휘가 많지도 않고 그 의미를 추측하고 넘어가는 것도 용이해서 별 문제가 되지 않을 것입니다. 반면 너무 어려운 원서를 골라 모르는 어휘가 지나치게 많이 등장한다면, 문맥에 따라 의미를 추측하는 것은 사실상 불가능합니다. 한 페이지(250단어)당 모르는 어휘가 10개가 넘는다면 지나치게 어려운 원서를 골랐다고 볼 수 있습니다. 수준에 맞는 원서를 고르고, 실력 향상에 맞춰 원서 수준도 높여가세요.

사실 어휘력을 쌓는다는 측면에서만 보면, 모르는 단어를 찾아보며 읽는 것도 좋은 방법입니다. 다만, 사전만 들여다보다 지치지 않도록 균형을 맞추는 것이 중요하겠지요. 만약 미리 누군가 어려운 단어를 정리해줬다면, 그보다 더 좋을 수는 없을 것입니다. (그래서 이런 원서 읽는 단어장이 있는 것이겠죠?)

Q. 이 원서가 너무 어렵게 느껴지는데… 계속 읽어야 할까요?

A. 어려워도 꼭 읽고 싶다는 생각이 드는 책이라면 계속 읽는 것이 좋지만, 그렇지 않은 책이라면 과감히 포기하는 것이 좋습니다. 원서 읽기를 통한 영어 공부에서 가장 중요한 것은 '스트레스 받지 않고 즐겁게' 읽는 것입니다. 어려운 원서로 스트레스만 받는다면, 꾸준히 읽지도 못하고 영어 실력도 향상되기 힘듭니다. 더 쉽고 관심 있는 책을 골라보세요.

Q. 제대로 이해하는 건지 걱정이 되는데, 번역서를 같이 보고 읽는 것은 어떤가요?

A. 추천하지 않습니다. 번역 역시 100% 완벽하다고 할 수 없을뿐더러, 영어를 한글로 바꿔야만 직성이 풀리는 좋지 않은 리딩 습관을 기를 수 있기 때문입니다.

번역된 책과 함께 읽기보다, '영화'와 함께 읽는 것을 추천합니다. 즉, 영화화 된 원서 혹은 영화 기반의 원서를 읽을 것이지요. 영화를 보고 해당 원서를 읽으면, 이미 대략적인 내용을 파악한 상태라 보다 수월하게 리딩 할 수 있기 때문입니다. 또 내용에 따른 전후 상황, 느낌과 분위기, 뉘앙스 등을 영화를 통해 파악했기 때문에 리딩 시에 '보다 폭넓은 이해'가 가능합니다.

'글을 읽는다'는 것은 단순히 '무슨 내용인지 안다'는 의미가 아닙니다. 왜 이런 상황에서 이런 이야기를 하는지, 등장인물은 어떤 감정으로 대화하고 있는지, 작가는 글을 통해 어떻게 효과적으로 정보를 전달하는지, 이런 점들까지 폭넓게 바라볼 수 있어야 '글을 제대로 읽는다'고 할 수 있습니다. 영화와 함께 원서를 읽는 것은 이런 깊이 있는 리딩 훈련이 자연스럽게 이루어지도록 도와줍니다.

Comprehension Quiz
Build Your Vocabulary
Crossword Puzzle

Comprehension Quiz

1. How many people are in Charlie's Family?

A. Six grownups

B. Just Charlie

C. Six grownups and Charlie

D. Six grownups, Charlies and His sister

2. Why was winter at Charlie's house so bad?

A. Because there was snow outside

B. Because he saw ghosts

C. Because his grandparents snored all night

D. Because freezing cold drafts blew across the floor all night

3. What did Mr. Bucket do?

A. He screwed the caps on the toothpaste tubes

B. He cooked cabbage

C. He made chocolate

D. He owned his chocolate factories

4. What was special about Sunday?

A. Everyone had steak

B. Everyone had a second helping

C. Only Charlie had seconds

D. Nobody had seconds

Chapter 1 **Here Comes Charlie**

5. How did Charlie eat his birthday chocolate?

A. He put it in a treasure box and never ate it

B. He nibbled little pieces each day for a month

C. He secretly ate the whole bar in one night

D. He melted and ate it

6. Who was Mr. Willy Wonka?

A. The owner of a palace

B. The president of a chocolate company

C. The world's finest inventor and maker of chocolates

7. What is not a characteristic of Wonka's factory?

A. It had huge iron gates

B. It had a high wall around it

C. It belched pink smoke from its chimneys

D. It made strange whizzing sounds

Comprehension Quiz

1. What is the meaning of the underlined part of 'They are <u>as shriveled as prunes</u>'?

A. As wrinkled as raisins

B. As old as time

C. As bony as skeletons

2. How many kinds of chocolate did Mr. Willy Wonka invent?

A. One kind

B. More ten kinds

C. More two hundred kinds

D. More two thousand kinds

3. What was special about Wonka's chocolate ice cream?

A. It would never melt

B. It would stay cold for hours

C. It would stay in an icebox

D. It would never be divied

4. Which was not a Wonka invention?

A. Marshmallows that taste like violets

B. Chewing gum that never loses its taste

C. Blue bird's eggs that leave a tiny pink sugary baby bird on your tongue

D. Chocolate frogs that jump out of windows

Chapter 2 **Mr. Willy Wonka's Factory**

5. Match the meanings.

A. Absurd •   • 1. Crazy

B. Completely dotty •   • 2. Impossible

C. Fantastic •   • 3. 100%

D. Absolutely •   • 4. Extraordinary

Comprehension Quiz

1. What did Prince Pondicherry want?

A. A marvelous chocolate bar

B. A chocolate palace

C. A chocolate cottage

D. His own chocolate factory

2. Where did the hot chocolate come from?

A. The garden hose

B. The dishwasher

C. The taps in the bathroom

Chapter 3 **Mr. Wonka and the Indian Prince**

3. Why did Willy Wonka say "...you'd better start eating right away?"

(A) _____

4. What does "...are you pulling my leg?" mean?

A. Are you telling me something that is not true?

B. Are you drawing my leg?

C. Are you touching me?

D. Are you picking a fight with me?

5. Who are the workers?

A. Ordinary people

B. Trained animals

C. Aliens

D. Oompa-Loompas

Comprehension Quiz

1. Why did the spies take jobs in the factories?

A. To break the machines

B. To steal the secret recipes

C. To take pictures

D. To make chocolate

2. Which chocolate maker did not send spies?

A. Slugworth

B. Fickelgruber

C. Prodnose

D. Cadbury

Chapter 4 **The Secret Workers**

3. How do the people know that there are workers?

A. The factory smells like chocolate

B. There are little shadows in the windows

C. The workers go home every night

D. The machines are whirring again

4. If no one comes in or out how does the chocolate get delivered?

A. By many workers in the chocolate factory

B. Chocolate buyers go into the factory and buy the chocolates themselves

C. Through a special trap door and by Post Office trucks

D. There are special robots delivering chocolates in the factory

5. How big are the shadows of the people in the factory?

A. No bigger than a grasshopper

B. No higher than Grandpa Joe's knee

C. No taller than a basketball player

D. No higher than a mountain

Comprehension Quiz

1. What do the children win if they find a golden ticket? (two answers)

A. A tour of the factory

B. A pet squirrel

C. Fizzy lifting drinks

D. A lifetime supply of chocolate

2. What do they think of a lifetime supply of chocolate?

A. Grandma Georgina •

B. Grandma Josephine •

• a. "They'd have to deliver them on a truck."

• b. "It makes me quite ill to think of it."

3. What does not glistening mean?

A. Shining

B. Reflecting

C. Sparkling

D. Dull

Chapter 5 **The Golden Tickets**

4. What does Grandpa George think of Charlie's chances of finding a golden ticket?

A. He has the same chance as the other children

B. He has no chance

C. He will get all five tickets

D. He will find a ticket in the snow

Build your Vocabulary

Chapter 1. Here Comes Charlie

- **draft** [dræft] *n.* 틈새 바람, 외풍; 도안, 밑그림; *vt.* 밑그림을 그리다, 설계하다
  A current of air that comes into a place in an undesirable way.

- **awful** [ɔ́:fəl] *a.* 지독한, 심한; (정도가) 대단한; 무서운
  Extremely bad or unpleasant.

- **toothpaste** [tú:θpèist] *n.* (크림 모양의) 치약
  A thick substance which you put on your toothbrush and use to clean your teeth.

- **proper** [prápər] *a.* 적당[타당]한; 예의 바른; 고유의
  The proper thing is the one that is correct or most suitable.

- **afford** [əfɔ́:rd] *vt.* …할 여유가 있다; 주다, 공급하다
  If you cannot afford something, you do not have enough money to pay for it.

- **a second helping** *idiom* 두 그릇째

- **tummy** [tʌ́mi] *n.* (유아어) 배(stomach)
  Your tummy is the part of the front of your body below your waist.

- **desperate** [déspərit] *a.* 막 가는; 필사적인; 절망적인
  (desperately *ad.* 필사적으로; 절망적으로)
  If you are desperate for something, you want or need it very much indeed.

- **long** [lɔ:ŋ] *a.* 긴, 오랜; *vi.* 간절히 바라다, 동경하다
  If you long for something, you want it very much.

- **slab** [slæb] *n.* 석판, 널빤지
  A slab of something is a thick, flat piece of it.

- **munch** [mʌntʃ] *v.* 우적우적 먹다
  If you munch food, you eat it by chewing it slowly, thoroughly, and rather noisily.

- **torture** [tɔ́:rtʃər] *n.* 고문, 고뇌; *vt.* 고문하다, 고통을 주다
  To torture someone means to cause them to suffer mental pain or anxiety.

- **occasion** [əkéiʒən] *n.* 경우, 때, 특별한 일, 기회
  A particular event or happening.

- **marvellous** [má:rvələs] (= marvelous) *a.* 놀라운, 믿기 어려운; (구어) 훌륭한
  Extremely good.

- **peel** [pi:l] *v.* (껍질을) 벗다, 벗기다
  To strip off an outer layer.

J ★ **nibble** [níbəl] *v.* 조금씩 물어뜯다, 갉아먹다; *n.* 조금씩 물어뜯기, 한 번 분량
  To eat something by biting very small pieces of it.

MJ ★ **enormous** [inɔ́:rməs] *a.* 막대한, 거대한
  Extremely large.

MJ ★ **tremendous** [triméndəs] *a.* 거대한, 대단한; 엄청난, 무서운
  You use tremendous to emphasize how strong a feeling or quality is, or how large an amount is.

M ★ **belch** [beltʃ] *vt.* 분출하다, 내뿜다; *vi.* 트림을 하다
  If a machine or chimney belches something such as smoke or fire, large amounts of smoke or fire come from it.

★ **whiz(z)** [hwiz] *n.* (속어) 명수, 명인; 윙, 씽, 핑 (공중을 가르는 소리)
  To move or do something very fast.

★ **scent** [sent] *n.* 냄새, 향기; *v.* 냄새 맡다
  If something scents a place or thing, it makes it smell pleasant.

★ **sniff** [snif] *v.* 코를 킁킁거리다; 콧방귀를 뀌며 말하다
  To speak in an unpleasant way, showing that you have a low opinion of something.

★ **gorgeous** [gɔ́:rdʒəs] *a.* 호화로운, 찬란한, 훌륭한
  Extremely beautiful or attractive.

Chapter 2. Mr. Willy Wonka's Factory

★ **cabbage** [kǽbidʒ] *n.* 양배추
  A cabbage is a round vegetable with green leaves that is usually eaten cooked.

MJ ★ **shrivel** [ʃrívəl] *v.* 주름(살)지다[게 하다], 줄어들다
  To become dry, smaller and covered with lines as if by crushing or folding, or to make something do this.

★ **prune** [pru:n] ① *vt.* (가지·뿌리 등을) 잘라내다, 치다 ② *n.* 서양 자두, 말린 자두
  A dried plum.

★ **bony** [bóuni] *a.* 뼈의, 뼈뿐인
  Very thin.

Build your Vocabulary

huddle [hʌ́dl] *v.* 붐비다, (떼 지어) 몰리다, 쌓아 올리다
To heap or crowd together closely.

doze [douz] *v.* 졸다 *n.* 졸기, 겉잠
To sleep lightly or for a short period, especially during the daytime.

good heavens *idiom* 큰일이군! (저런!)

extraordinary [ikstrɔ́:rdənèri] *a.* 대단한, 비상한, 비범한; 터무니없는
Very unusual, special, unexpected or strange.

delicate [délikət] *a.* 섬세한; 미묘한; 민감한; 허약한, 가냘픈
Someone who is delicate is not healthy and strong, and becomes ill easily.

the four corners of the earth
[성서] 지구 끝, 지구의 구석구석 (이사야서 11:12)
To refer to places that are a long way from each other.

up one's sleeve *idiom* 몰래 준비해 두고[둔]
If you have something up your sleeve, you have an idea or plan which you have not told anyone about.

runny [rʌ́ni] *a.* 흐르는 경향이 있는, 액체 비슷한, 점액을 잘 분비하는
Something that is runny is more liquid than usual or than was intended.

absurd [əbsə́:rd] *a.* 불합리한, 부조리한, 터무니없는
ridiculous or unreasonable; foolish in an amusing way.

feathery [féðəri] *a.* 깃이 난; 깃으로 덮인; 깃털 같은; 가벼운; 천박한
Feathery is used to describe things that are soft and light.

pop [pɔp] *v.* 불쑥 움직이다; 팡하고 쏘다[꺼내다]; 뻥하고 터지다
If someone or something pops up, they appear in a place unexpectedly.

gobble [gábəl] *vt.* 게걸스레 먹다; 꿀떡 삼키다
If you gobble food, you eat it quickly and greedily.

sugary [ʃúgəri] *a.* 설탕의[같은], 설탕으로 된; 단
Sugary food or drink contains a lot of sugar.

chuckle [tʃʌ́kl] *vi.* 낄낄 웃다; (혼자서) 기뻐하다; *n.* 낄낄 웃음, 미소
To laugh quietly.

- **dotty** [dɔ́ti] *a.* 점이 많은; 머리가 돈; 휘청대는, 흔들리는
  Slightly strange or mentally ill.

Chapter 3. Mr. Wonka and the Indian Prince

- ★ **colossal** [kəlásəl] *a.* 거대한, (구어) 어마어마한, 굉장한
  If you describe something as colossal, you are emphasizing that it is very large.

- **ceiling** [síːliŋ] *n.* 천장
  A ceiling is the horizontal surface that forms the top part or roof inside a room.

- **tap** [tæp] *v.* ① 가볍게 두드리다 ② *n.* (수도 등의) 꼭지, 마개
  A tap is a device that controls the flow of a liquid or gas from a pipe or container.

- **nibble** [níbəl] *v.* 조금씩 물어뜯다, 갉아먹다; *n.* 조금씩 물어뜯기, 한 번 분량
  To eat something by biting very small pieces of it.

- **lick** [lik] *v.* 핥다; 날름거리다; (구어) 때리다; *n.* 핥기
  To move the tongue across the surface of something.

- **doze** [douz] *v.* 졸다 *n.* 졸기, 겉잠
  When you doze, you sleep lightly or for a short period, especially during the daytime.

- **pull a person's leg** *idiom* …을 놀리다, 속이다, 희롱하다
  If you are pulling someone's leg, you are teasing them by telling them something shocking or worrying as a joke.

- **stammer** [stǽmər] *v.* 말을 더듬다, 더듬으며 말하다
  If you stammer, you speak with difficulty, hesitating and repeating words or sounds.

Chapter 4. The Secret Workers

- **recipe** [résəpìː] *n.* 조리법, 요리법; 처방전; 방법, 비결
  A list of ingredients and a set of instructions that tell you how to cook something.

- **tear** [tɛər] ① *n.* 눈물 ② (tore-torn) *v.* 찢다, 째다
  If you tear paper, cloth, or another material, you pull it into two pieces or you pull it so that a hole appears in it.

- **beard** [biərd] *n.* 턱수염
  The hair that some men allow to grow on the lower part of their face.

Build your Vocabulary

- **fasten** [fǽsn] *v.* 묶다, 고정시키다, 채우다
  To attach something firmly to another object.

- **desert** [dezə:rt] *v.* 버리다, 돌보지 않다 (deserted *a.* 인적이 끊긴)
  To leave a place or person, intending not to return.

   whirr [hwə:r] (= whir) *v.* 씽 소리 내며 날다[회전하다, 움직이다]; *n.* 씽 하는 소리
  When something whirrs, it makes a series of low sounds so quickly that they seem like one continuous sound.

- **marvellous** [má:rvələs] (= marvelous) *a.* 놀라운, 믿기 어려운; (구어) 훌륭한
  Extremely good.

- **lit** [lit] *a.* 불 켜진, 빛나는 (light의 과거 · 과거분사)
  Lighted.

- **furnace** [fə́:rnis] *n.* 노(爐); 아궁이, 화덕
  A furnace is a container or enclosed space in which a very hot fire is made.

- **frost** [frɔ́:st] *n.* 서리 *v.* 서리로 덮다, 서리가 앉다
  When there is frost or a frost, the temperature outside falls below freezing point and the ground becomes covered in ice crystals.

- **absurd** [əbsə́:rd] *a.* 불합리한, 부조리한, 터무니없는
  ridiculous or unreasonable; foolish in an amusing way.

- **trap** [træp] *n.* 덫, 함정; *v.* 덫을 놓다
  A trap is a device which is placed somewhere or a hole which is dug somewhere in order to catch animals or birds.

Chapter 5. The Gorden Tickets

   smooth out *idiom* …의 주름을 펴다
  If you smooth out a problem or difficulty, you solve it, especially by talking to the people concerned.

   mind (you) *idiom* 알겠니, 잘 들어 둬 (양보 또는 조건 제시에 따르는 삽입 문구)

- **tour** [tuər] *n.* 관광 여행, (공장 · 시설 등의) 견학, 시찰; *v.* 관광 여행하다; 여행하다
  A visit to a place or area, especially one during which you look round the place or area and learn about it.

Chapter 1-5

- ✱ **mutter** [mʌ́tər] *vi.* 중얼거리다, 낮게 투덜대다
  To speak quietly so that your voice is difficult to hear.

- ★ **glisten** [glísn] *vi.* 반짝이다, 빛나다
  If something glistens, it shines, usually because it is wet or oily.

Crossword Puzzle

Use the clues and the words in the box to complete the crossword puzzle.

doze	draft	huddle	awful	gobble	marvellous
munch	nibble	colossal	torture	absurd	extraordinary
shrivel	glisten	delicate	mutter	desperate	tremendous

Across

3   To sleep lightly or for a short period, especially during the daytime.
4   To heap or crowd together closely.
7   Extremely bad or unpleasant.
12 Very unusual, special, unexpected or strange.
13 If something _____s, it shines, usually because it is wet or oily.
14 To eat something by biting very small pieces of it.
15 Ridiculous or unreasonable; foolish in an amusing way.
16 Extremely good.

Down

1   To cause them to suffer mental pain or anxiety.
2   Someone who is delicate is not healthy and strong, and becomes ill easily.
3   A current of air that comes into a place in an undesirable way.
5   If you are _____ for something, you want or need it very much indeed.
6   To speak quietly so that your voice is difficult to hear.
8   If you describe something as _____, you are emphasizing that it is very large.
9   To become dry, smaller and covered with lines as if by crushing or folding, or to make something do this.
10 If you _____ food, you eat it by chewing it slowly, thoroughly, and rather noisily.
11 Very great in amount or level, or extremely good.
13 If you _____ food, you eat it quickly and greedily.

Comprehension Quiz

1. What does Augustus Gloop look like?(two answers)

A. Great flabby folds of fat bulged out from every part of his body

B. He was talking very fast and very loudly to everyone

C. His eyes were glued to the screen in which one bunch of gangsters was shooting up another bunch of gangsters with machine guns

D. His face was like a monstrous ball of dough with two small greedy currant eyes

2. Augustus' hobby is _____.

3. What does the Augustus' mother think? (two answers)

A. He needs the vitamins in chocolate

B. Eating healthy is important

C. Eating is better than shooting zip guns

D. Eating is better than studying

4. Who tried to cheat?

(A)_____

(B)_____

(C)_____

Chapter 6 **The First Two Finder**

5. What is not true about Mr. Salt?

A. He is rich

B. He had the peanut workers open hundreds of thousands of Wonka bars

C. He is spoiled

D. He loves Veruca

6. What do the grandparents think of Veruca Salt? (two answers)

A. She needs a real good spanking

B. She will be a famous actress

C. She is worse than the fat boy

D. She will be a good girl when she grows up

Comprehension Quiz

1. What is the name of the candy bar?

(A)_____

2. When Charlie touched the candy bar what kind of noises did it make?

A. Crunchy noises

B. Sharp crackly noises

C. High screeching noises

D. Muddy squishy noises

Chapter 7 **Charlie's Birthday**

3. Why did Grandma Georgina say "The thing to remember··· is that whatever happens, you'll still have the bar of candy."?

A. To dissuade Charlie from opening the present

B. To assure Charlie that he can get a Golden Ticket

C. To prepare Charlie for disappointment

D. To cheer Charlie up to get some money for a Chocolate bar

4. Why were the parents and grandparents as tense as Charlie?

A. Because there was still a small chance that the ticket was in Charlie's chocolate bar

B. Because they wanted to eat Charlie's chocolate bar

C. Because they were afraid that Charlie would cry when he found no golden ticket in the chocolate bar

D. Because they were afraid that Charlie would eat the chocolate bar in front of them

5. Why did Charlie want to share his chocolate bar with his family?

A. Because he did not find a golden ticket

B. Because he was disappointed, he did not want to eat it

C. Because it was dirty

D. Because he knew that his family was as disappointed as he was and wanted to make them feel better

Comprehension Quiz

1. What is Violet's problem?

A. She is pretty

B. She is obnoxious

C. She is harsh

D. She is happy

2. Where does Violet leave her gum at mealtimes?

A. In the elevator

B. On the bed post

C. In the trash can

D. Behind her ear

Chapter 8 **Two More Golden Tickets Found**

3. What is Mike's problem?

(A)_____

4. What is Mike's favorite kind of program?

A. Romantic Comedies

B. Comedy Showes

C. Gangster Films

D. Reality Showes

5. Which one is not a way that gangsters fight?

A. Shooting guns

B. Fighting with knives

C. Fist fighting

D. Flying attack helicopters

Comprehension Quiz

1. What did Grandpa Joe have under the pillow?

A. A chocolate bar

B. Candy

C. An ancient leather purse

D. A screte recipe

2. What did Grandpa Joe call a single silver six pence?

A. My secret toad

B. My secret hoard

C. My secret money

3. What was the name of the chocolate that Charlie bought with Grandpa Joe's six pence?

A. Hair Toffee

B. Butter Scotch and Chocolate

C. Wonka's Nutty Crunch Surprise

D. Wonka's Chocolate

Chapter 9 **Grandpa Joe Takes a Gamble**

4. How did Grandpa Joe and Charlie open the bar of candy?

A. They tore the corner off

B. They opened it with a knife

C. They broke it open

D. They tore the paper by turns

Comprehension Quiz

1. The family had two vital problems. What are they? (two answers)

A. Trying to keep warm

B. Trying to do laundry

C. Trying to get enough to eat

D. Trying to get a golden ticket

2. What happened when the toothpaste factory went bust?

(A)_____

3. How did Mr. Bucket make a few pennies?

A. Shoveling snow

B. Managing the peanut business

C. Selling gum

D. Working at a chocolate factory

Chapter 10 **The Family Begins to Starve**

4. What did Charlie do in front of the chocolate factory?

A. He tried to eat the smell of the chocolate

B. He looked in the windows

C. He bought some chocolate bars from Mr. Wonka

D. He yelled for Mr. Wonka to open the gate and give him some chocolate

5. Why did Grandpa George say that Charlie is a fine fellow? (two answers)

A. Because Charlie cleaned the house

B. Because Charlie listened to the grandparents' stories

C. Because Charlie would not eat other people's food

D. Because Charlie was considerate

6. What did Charlie find in the snow?

(A)_____

7. What did Charlie plan to do with the money? (two answers)

A. Buy and eat a chocolate bar

B. Give the rest of the money to his mother

C. Buy meat for the family

D. Buy a hen that could lay eggs

Build your Vocabulary

6. The First Two Finder

- MJ **flabby** [flǽbi] *a.* (몸에 살이 쪄서) 흐늘흐늘하는, 축 늘어진
  Soft and fat, weak.

- MJ ★ **bulge** [bʌldʒ] *v.* 부풀다, 불룩해지다, 튀어나오다, 부풀리다
  If something such as a person's stomach bulges, it sticks out.

- ★ **dough** [dou] *n.* 굽지 않는 빵, 가루 반죽; 반죽 덩어리
  Dough is a fairly firm mixture of flour, water, and sometimes also fat and sugar.

- **curranty** [kə́:rənti] currant(*n.* 건포도)의 형용사 형태: '아주 작은'
  Currants are small dried black grapes, used especially in cakes.

- ★ **peer** [piər] *vi.* 자세히 보다, 응시하다
  If you peer at something, you look at it very hard.

- **hooligan** [húːligən] *n.* 깡패; 훌리건 (축구 시합 등에서 난동부리는 관객)
  If you describe people as hooligans, you are critical of them because they behave in a noisy and violent way in a public place.

- **zip gun** *n.* (미·속어) 수제 권총

- M ‡ **revolt** [rivóult] *v.* 비위가 상하다[게 하다]; 반항[배반]하다; *n.* 반란, 폭동
  To make someone feel unpleasantly shocked or disgusted.

- J **repulsive** [ripʌ́lsiv] *a.* 되쫓아버리는, 박차는; 쌀쌀한; 싫은, 불쾌한
  Extremely unpleasant or unacceptable.

- **spree** [spriː] *n.* 흥청거림, 법석댐; 연회; 주연; 탐닉; *vi.* 흥겹게 마시고 떠들다
  A short period of doing a particular, usually enjoyable, activity much more than is usual.

- J ★ **frantic** [frǽntik] *a.* 광란의, 미친 듯 날뛰는 (frantically *ad.* 미친 듯이)
  Behaving in a wild and uncontrolled way.

- M ‡ **precious** [préʃəs] *a.* 귀중한, 가치가 있는, 비싼
  Of great value because of being rare, expensive or important.

- J ★ **glint** [glint] *v.* 반짝이다, 빛나다; *n.* 반짝임, 섬광
  If something glints, it produces or reflects a quick flash of light.

Chapter 6-10

piggy [pígi] *n.* 돼지 새끼
A baby pig.

J ‡ **amidst** [əmídst] *prep.* (= amid) …의 한복판에, 한창 …하는 중에
If something is amidst other things, it is surrounded by them.

‡ **dagger** [dǽgər] *n.* 단도, 단검; *vt.* 단도로 찌르다, … 에 칼표를 하다
A dagger is a weapon like a knife with two sharp edges.

★ **duchess** [dʌ́tʃis] *n.* 공작부인, 여 공작
A woman who has the same rank as a duke, or who is a duke's wife or widow.

‡ **beam** [bi:m] *vi.* 빛을 발하다; 밝게 미소짓다
If you say that someone is beaming, you mean that they have a big smile on their face.

feller [félər] *n.* (구어) (= fellow) 동무, 친구
The people who you work with, do things with, or who are like you in some way.

‡ **joint** [dʒɔint] *n.* 이음매, 관절; (미·속어) 건물, 장소; *a.* 공동의, 합동의
A place where people go for entertainment and which often has a bad reputation.

‡‡ **shell** [ʃel] *n.* 껍데기; *v.* 껍데기를 벗기다[싸다, 깔다]; 껍데기가 벗겨지다
The hard outer covering of eggs, nuts, or seeds.

‡ **roast** [roust] *v.* 굽다, 그을리다, 뜨겁게 하다
When you roast meat or other food, you cook it by dry heat in an oven or over a fire.

‡‡ **salt** [sɔ:lt] *v.* 소금을 치다, 간을 맞추다; *n.* 소금
To add salt to or put salt on something.

M **yank** [jæŋk] *v.* (구어) 확 잡아당기다
To pull something forcefully with a quick movement.

‡ **vow** [vau] *n.* 맹세, 서약, 서원 *v.* 맹세하다, 서약하다
If you vow to do something, you make a serious promise or decision that you will do it.

★ **spank** [spæŋk] *v.* 찰싹 때리다; *n.* 찰싹 때리기
To hit a child with the hand, usually several times on the bottom as a punishment.

M ‡‡ **spoil** [spɔil] *vt.* 망쳐놓다, 손상하다; 버릇없이 기르다
If you spoil something, you prevent it from being successful or satisfactory.

Build your Vocabulary

7. Charlie's Birthday

- **scrumptious** [skrʌmpʃəs] *a.* (구어) 몹시 즐거운, 멋진, 굉장한
  If you describe food as scrumptious, you mean that it tastes extremely good.

- **prop** [prɔp] *n.* 지주, 버팀목; *v.* 받치다, 버티다; 지지하다
  If you prop an object on or against something, you support it by putting something underneath it or by resting it somewhere.

- **stroke** [strouk] ① *n.* 타격, 일격, 치기 ② *vt.* 쓰다듬다, 어루만지다
  If you stroke someone or something, you move your hand slowly and gently over them.

- **crackly** [krǽkli] *a.* 파삭파삭[바삭바삭]한
  Something that is crackly, especially a recording or broadcast, has or makes a lot of short, harsh noises.

- **ridiculous** [ridíkjələs] *a.* 웃기는, 우스꽝스러운
  Stupid or unreasonable and deserving to be laughed at.

- **crane** [krein] *v.* (목을) 쭉 내밀다; 달아 올리다
  To stretch in order to look at something.

- **scraggy** [skrǽgi] *a.* 말라빠진, 빈약한, 울퉁불퉁한
  Very thin, especially so that the bones stick out.

- **intent** [intént] *a.* 집중된, 열중하여 (intently *ad.* 골똘하게, 여념 없이, 오로지)
  Giving all your attention to something.

- **shrug** [ʃrʌg] *v.* (어깨를) 으쓱하다
  To raise up and drop the shoulders briefly as an indication of doubt, indifference, etc.

8. Two More Golden Tickets Found

- **jostle** [dʒɑ́sl] *v.* (난폭하게) 떠밀다, 헤치고 나아가다; *n.* 서로 밀치기, 부딪침
  To knock or push roughly against someone in order to move past them or get more space when you are in a crowd of people

- **ferocious** [fəróuʃəs] *a.* 사나운; (구어) 지독한, 맹렬한
  (ferociously *ad.* 사납게, 잔인하게, 지독하게)
  Fierce and violent.

munch [mʌntʃ] *v.* 우적우적 먹다
If you munch food, you eat it by chewing it slowly, thoroughly, and rather noisily.

wedge [wedʒ] *vt.* 밀어 넣다, 끼워 넣다; *n.* 쐐기
To force something firmly into a narrow space.

trample [trǽmpəl] *v.* 짓밟다, 밟아 뭉개다, 무시하다
To step heavily on something or someone, causing damage or injury.

mob [mɔb] *n.* 군중, 폭도
A large noisy crowd, especially one that is angry and violent.

bedpost [bédpòust] *n.* (네 귀의) 침대 기둥, 침대다리
One of the four corner poles that support a bed.

gooey [gúːi] *a.* 끈적끈적한, 들러붙는; *n.* 끈적거리는 것, 당밀
Soft and sticky.

racket [rǽkit] *n.* 떠드는 소리, 큰 소리, 야단법석; *n.* 라켓
An unpleasant loud continuous noise.

beastly [bíːstli] *a.* 짐승 같은; 잔인한; 더러운 *ad.* 몹시, 아주
Unkind or unpleasant.

despicable [déspikəbəl] *a.* 야비한, 비열한
Very unpleasant or bad, causing strong feelings of dislike.

cram [kræm] *vt.* 억지로 채워 넣다, 밀어 넣다
To force a lot of things into a small space, or to do many things in a short period of time.

glue [gluː] *n.* 아교, 끈적끈적한 물건, 접착제; *vt.* 아교로 붙이다, …에 집중하다
If you glue one object to another, you stick them together using glue.

bunch [bʌntʃ] *n.* 다발, 송이, 떼; *v.* 다발로 만들다; (한 떼로) 모으다, 모이다
A group of people.

leap [liːp] (leapt–leapt) *v.* 껑충 뛰다; 뛰어넘다; *n.* 뜀, 도약, 비약, 급변
To make a large jump or sudden movement, usually from one place to another.

whiz-banger *n.* 정말 멋진 것 (whiz-bang *a.* 일류의, 최고의)

Build your Vocabulary

crummy [krʌ́mi] *a.* 초라한, 값싼, 지저분한
Of very bad quality.

stiletto [stilétou] *n.* 양날 단도, 송곳칼; 구멍 냄; *vt.* 단검으로 찌르다[죽이다]

★ **knuckle** [nʌ́kəl] *n.* 손가락 관절[마디]; *v.* 손가락 마디로 치다
One of the joints in the hand where your fingers bend, especially where your fingers join on to the main part of your hand.

★ **duster** [dʌ́stər] *n.* 먼지 터는 사람, 청소부; 먼지떨이, 총채
A duster is a cloth which you use for removing dust from furniture, ornaments, or other objects.

knuckle duster *n.* (격투할 때 손가락 관절에 끼우는) 쇳조각
A metal weapon which is worn over the knuckles and is intended to increase the injuries caused when hitting a person.

J ★ **brat** [bræt] *n.* (경멸적) 선머슴, 개구쟁이
A child, especially one who behaves badly.

MJ ☆ **nasty** [nǽsti] *a.* 더러운, 불쾌한, 몹시 싫은; 심술궂은, 험악한
Bad or very unpleasant.

9. Grandpa Joe Takes a Gamble

J ★ **beckon** [békən] *v.* 손짓[고갯짓, 몸짓]으로 부르다, 신호하다
To move your hand or head in a way that tells someone to come nearer.

J ☆ **tiptoe** [típtòu] *n.* 발끝; *vi.* 발끝으로 걷다; 발돋움하다
On your toes with the heel of your foot lifted off the ground.

J ☆ **sly** [slai] *a.* 은밀한, 음흉한; 익살맞은 (slyly *ad.* 음흉하게, 장난스럽게)
A sly look or expression shows that you know something that other people do not know.

rummage [rʌ́midʒ] *v.* 샅샅이 뒤지다. (찾기 위하여) 마구 뒤적거리다
To search for something by moving things around carelessly and looking into, under and behind them.

MJ ☆ **clutch** [klʌtʃ] *vt.* 꽉 잡다, 붙들다
To take or try to take hold of something tightly.

Chapter 6-10

- M **tip** [tip] *v.* 기울이다, 뒤집어엎다
  To (cause to) move so that one side is higher than another side.

- ★ **hoard** [hɔːrd] *n.* 저장물, 축적
  To collect large amounts of something and keep it in a safe, often secret, place.

- ‡ **fling** [fliŋ] (flung–flung) *vt.* 던지다, 내던지다
  If you fling something somewhere, you throw it there using a lot of force.

- M **splutter** [splʌ́tər] (= sputter) *vi.* 푸푸 소리를 내다; 입에서 침을 튀기다
  To works or burns in an uneven way and makes a series of soft popping sounds.

- ‡ **tremble** [trémbəl] *v.* 떨다, 떨리다
  To shake slightly, usually because you are cold or frightened.

- ★ **fumble** [fʌ́mbəl] *vi.* 손으로 더듬어 찾다
  If you fumble for something, you try and reach for it or hold it in a clumsy way.

- M ★ **giggle** [gígəl] *v.* 킥킥 웃다
  To laugh repeatedly in a quiet but uncontrolled and childish way.

- ★ **peal** [piːl] *n.* 울림
  A long loud sound or series of sounds, especially of laughter or thunder.

- **heck** [hek] *n.* 지옥(hell의 완곡한 말)
  Used to say that you will do something although you know you should not do it.

10. The Family Begins to Starve

- ‡ **flake** [fleik] *n.* 얇은 조각, 박편
  A small thin piece of something, especially if it has come from a layered surface.

- ‡ **drift** [drift] *v.* 표류하다, 떠돌다
  To move slowly with no control over direction.

- ‡ **gale** [geil] *n.* 질풍, 강풍; (pl.) (감정·웃음 등의) 폭발, 돌발적인 소리
  A very strong wind.

- J ‡ **huddle** [hʌ́dl] *v.* 붐비다, (떼 지어) 몰리다, 쌓아 올리다
  To heap or crowd together closely.

Build your Vocabulary

★ **crave** [kreiv] *v.* 열망하다, 갈망하다, 간절히 원하다
A strong or uncontrollable desire.

ravenous [rǽvənəs] *a.* 게걸스럽게 먹는; 몹시 굶주린, 탐욕스러운
Extremely hungry.

복습 **nibble** [níbəl] *v.* 조금씩 물어뜯다, 갉아먹다; *n.* 조금씩 물어뜯기, 한 번 분량
To eat something by taking a lot of small bites.

bust [bʌst] *v.* 파열하다, 깨다, 부수다
If you bust something, you break it or damage it so badly that it cannot be used.

‡ **shovel** [ʃʌ́vəl] *n.* 삽; *v.* …을 삽으로 뜨다[파다], 삽으로 일하다
If you shovel earth, coal, or snow, you lift and move it with a shovel.

★ **trudge** [trʌdʒ] *v.* 무거운 발걸음으로 걷다, 터벅터벅 걷다
To walk slowly with a lot of effort, especially over a difficult surface or while carrying something heavy.

‡ **cruel** [krúːəl] *a.* 잔혹한, 무자비한
Extremely unkind and unpleasant and causing pain to people or animals intentionally.

‡ **recess** [riːses] *n.* 쉼, 휴식; 쉬는 시간
A temporary break from work.

★ **exhaustion** [igzɔ́ːstʃən] *n.* 극도의 피로, 기진맥진
To make someone extremely tired.

★ **gutter** [gʌ́tər] *n.* 배수구, 도랑
The edge of a road where rain flows away.

‡ **vague** [veig] *a.* 어렴풋한, 막연한 (vaguely *ad.* 모호하게, 막연하게)
Not clearly expressed, known, described or decided.

★ **curb** [kəːrb] *n.* 연석(차도에서 인도 사이의 약간 높은 턱); 재갈; 구속
The edge of a raised path nearest the road.

crunch [krʌntʃ] *n.* (의성어) 우두둑 부서지는 소리; *v.* 우두둑 깨물다[부수다]
A noise like the sound of something being crushed.

MJ ★ **crouch** [krautʃ] *v.* 몸을 구부리다, 쭈그리다, 웅크리다
To bend your knees and lower yourself so that you are close to the ground and leaning forward slightly.

Chapter 6-10

* **damp** [dæmp] *a.* 축축한
Slightly wet, especially in a way that is not pleasant or comfortable.

* **shiver** [ʃívər] *v.* (추위·공포로) 후들후들 떨다
To shake slightly because you are cold or frightened.

* **gaze** [geiz] *vi.* 응시하다, 지켜보다; *n.* 응시, 주시
To look at something or someone for a long time, especially in surprise, admiration or because you are thinking about something else.

luscious [lʌ́ʃəs] *a.* 감미로운, 달콤한
Having a pleasant sweet taste or containing a lot of juice.

Crossword Puzzle

Use the clues and the words in the box to complete the crossword puzzle.

bulge	fling	crane	shrug	repulsive	clutch	luscious
tip	spoil	wedge	trudge	crouch	beam	ridiculous
roast	leap	cram	precious	beastly	vague	splutter
peer	beckon	hooligan	flabby			

Chapter 6-10

Across

5   If something such as a person's stomach _____s, it sticks out.
7   To throw something somewhere using a lot of force.
8   To raise up and drop the shoulders briefly as an indication of doubt, indifference, etc.
9   Unkind or unpleasant.
11 If you describe something or someone as _____, you mean that they are horrible and disgusting and you want to avoid them.
13 To (cause to) move so that one side is higher than another side.
14 To move your hand or head in a way that tells someone to come nearer.
15 Not clearly expressed, known, described or decided.
16 To make a large jump or sudden movement, usually from one place to another.
18 To force a lot of things into a small space, or to do many things in a short period of time.
19 To prevent something from being successful or satisfactory.
20 To stretch in order to look at something.

Down

1   To bend your knees and lower yourself so that you are close to the ground and leaning forward slightly.
2   To walk slowly with a lot of effort, especially over a difficult surface or while carrying something heavy.
3   To force something firmly into a narrow space.
4   Of great value because of being rare, expensive or important.
6   If you describe people as _____s, you are critical of them because they behave in a noisy and violent way in a public place.
7   Soft and fat, weak.
8   To works or burns in an uneven way and makes a series of soft popping sounds.
9   If you say that someone is _____ing, you mean that they have a big smile on their face.
10 Having a pleasant sweet taste or containing a lot of juice.
11 Stupid or unreasonable and deserving to be laughed at.
12 To look at something very hard.
17 To cook meat or other food by dry heat in an oven or over a fire.
18 To take or try to take hold of something tightly.

Comprehension Quiz

1. What does not "Charlie went on wolfing the candy." mean?

A. He looked like a wolf

B. He was eating fast

C. He was eating large bites

D. He was not chewing very much

Chapter 11 **The Miracle**

2. Why didn't Charlie move when he first saw the golden ticket?

A. He was sad

B. He wanted to sell it

C. He got angry

D. He was happy

3. What did the adults offer to give him for the ticket?

A. A new factory

B. A new house

C. A chocolate shop

D. Five hundred dollars

4. Who saved Charlie from the mob?

A. Mr. Wonka

B. Grandpa Joe

C. The shopkeeper

D. Oompa-Lommpas

Comprehension Quiz

1. Put the events in the proper order.

(- - - -)

A. The shopkeeper saved Charlie from the mob

B. Charlie bought two candy bars

C. Charlie ran all of the way home

D. Charlie found the golden ticket

E. Charlie found a dollar bill in the snow

2. What does Charlie not have to do to get ready to go to Wonka's factory?

A. Wash his face

B. Comb his hair

C. Study about chocolates

D. Scrub his hands

Chapter 12 **What It Said on the Golden Ticket**

3. Why does Grandpa Joe go with Charlie?

A. He is the tallest

B. He knows the most about the factory

C. He has the most money

D. He is the most healthy

4. What reaction does not happen when Grandpa Joe looks at the golden ticket?

A. He yells Yippeee

B. He smiles

C. He throws his soup at Charlie

D. He does a victory dance in his pajamas

5. Why did Charlie go to bed late?

A. Because many reporters stayed in his house until nearly midnight

B. Because he had a party with his family

C. Because he considered whether to sell the ticket or not until midnight

D. Because he was so happy that couldn't sleep until late

*Chapter 13 No Questions

Comprehension Quiz

1. What animal did Wonka look like?

A. He looked like a sneaky cat from the street

B. He looked like a loyal dog from a fire station

C. He looked like a noble eagle from a mountain

D. He looked like a quick clever squirrel from the park

2. Why does Wonka have to keep his factory so warm?

A. Because Mr. Wonka can't stand the cold

B. Because the workers are used to an extremely hot climate

C. Because Wonka's special chocolates are made at high temperatures

D. Becuase chocolates are frozen at low temperatures

Chapter 14 **Mr. Willy Wonka**

3. What could Grandpa Joe smell in the factory? (two answers)

A. Roasting coffee

B. Melting chocolate

C. Roasting meat

D. Melting ice

4. What did The factory look like?

A. A doghouse

B. A lion's den

C. A monkey's tree

D. A rabbit's warren

5. Why do the passages slope downwards? (two answers)

A. it is easier to see the sky

B. it is bigger

C. it is easier to build

D. it is prettier

Comprehension Quiz

1. How much chocolate is in the river?

(A)_____

2. What do the glass pipes do?

A. They mix the chocolate

B. They squeeze the juice of the enormous blueberry

C. They take the chocolate to the other rooms in the factory as needed

D. They send a real bar of chocolate whizzing through the air in tiny pieces

Chapter 15 **The Chocolate Room**

3. Name four words that mean flabbergasted.

(A)_____

(B)_____

(C)_____

(D)_____

4. What is "swudge"?

(A)_____

5. What are Oompa-Loompas like? (two answers)

A. They are red

B. They have funny long hair

C. They are knee high

D. They have only three fingers on each hand

Build your Vocabulary

11. The Miracle

- MJ 볼 **bulge** [bʌldʒ] *v.* 부풀다, 불룩해지다, 튀어나오다, 부풀리다
  To stick out in a round shape.

- M 볼 **cram** [kræm] *vt.* 억지로 채워 넣다, 밀어 넣다
  To force a lot of things into a small space, or to do many things in a short period of time.

- M ‡ **sheer** [ʃiər] *a.* 얇은, 순수한, 섞이지 않은; 깎아지른 듯한; *ad.* 완전히, 순전히
  Used to emphasize how very great, important or powerful a quality or feeling is.

- ★ **blissful** [blísfəl] *a.* 즐거운, 더 없이 행복한 (blissfully *ad.* 즐겁게, 기쁨에 겨워)
  Extremely or completely happy.

- **sonny** [sʌ́ni] *n.* (구어) 아가야, 얘(소년·연소자에 대한 친근한 호칭)

- **gut-ache** *n.* 배탈, 뱃속이 탈나는 것 (gut *n.* 소화관, 창자 + ache *n.* 아픔, 쑤심)

- ‡ **wolf** [wulf] *vt.* …을 게걸스럽게 먹다. 정신없이 먹다
  To eat a large amount of food very quickly.

- ‡ **fit** [fit] ① *v.* 끼우다, 맞게 하다, 적합하다 *a.* 적합한 ② *n.* 발작, 경련
  If someone has a fit they suddenly lose consciousness and their body makes uncontrollable movements.

- J ‡ **cluster** [klʌ́stər] *v.* 집중 발생하다; 밀집하다[시키다]; 떼 짓다[짓게 하다]
  If people cluster together, they gather together in a small group.

- ‡ **envious** *a.* 시기심이 강한; 질투하는, 샘내는
  If you are envious of someone, you want something that they have.

- ★ **dizzy** [dizi] *a.* 현기증 나는, 아찔한
  To feel as if everything is spinning round and being unable to balance.

- ‡ **peculiar** [pikjúːljər] *a.* 기묘한, 이상한; 특이한, 눈에 띄는
  Unusual and strange, sometimes in an unpleasant way.

- MJ **thump** [θʌmp] *v.* (심장이) 두근두근 뛰다; *n.* 탁, 쿵 (소리)
  To hit someone with your fist (= closed hand), or to hit something and cause a noise.

Chapter 11-15

12. What It Said on the Golden Ticket

- MJ ✱ **clatter** [klǽtər] *n.* 덜거덕거리는 소리; *v.* 달가닥달가닥 울리다
  To make continuous loud noises by hitting hard objects against each other, or to cause objects to do this.

- ✱ **verdict** [və́ːrdikt] *n.* 판단, 의견, 결정
  An opinion or decision made after judging the facts that are given, especially one made at the end of a trial.

- ✱ **pupil** [pjúːpəl] ① *n.* 학생, 제자 ② 눈동자, 동공
  The circular black area in the centre of your eye, through which light enters.

- ✱ **whatsoever** [hwÀtsouévər] *a.* (부정·의문문에서) 조금의 …도 (없는)
  Used after a negative phrase to add emphasis to the idea that is being expressed.

- MJ ✱ **leap** [liːp] (leapt-leapt) *v.* 껑충 뛰다; 뛰어넘다; *n.* 뜀, 도약; 비약, 급변
  To make a large jump or sudden movement, usually from one place to another.

- ✱ **hooray** [hu(ː)réi] (= hurrah) *int., n., vi.* 만세(를 부르다)
  People sometimes shout 'Hooray!' when they are very happy and excited about something.

- **cripes** [kraips] *int.* (속어) 저런, 이것 참
  An expression of surprise.

- **dervish** [də́ːrviʃ] *n.* 회교 금욕파의 수도사
  A member of a Muslim religious group which has an energetic dance as part of its worship.

- ✱ **hammer** [hǽmər] *v.* (망치로) 두들겨 펴다
  To hit or kick something with a lot of force.

- **jet-black** [dʒétblǽk] *a.* 흑색색의, 새까만
  Completely black.

- ✱ **tremendous** [triméndəs] *a.* 거대한, 대단한; 엄청난, 무서운
  Very great in amount or level, or extremely good.

- MJ ✱ **morsel** [mɔ́ːrsəl] *n.* 가벼운 식사, 맛난 음식
  A very small piece of food.

Build your Vocabulary

mystic [místik] *a.* 신비로운
Someone who attempts to be united with God through prayer.

entrance [éntrəns] *vt.* 황홀하게 하다, 도취시키다
If something or someone entrances you, they cause you to feel delight and wonder, often so that all your attention is taken up and you cannot think about anything else.

intrigue [intríːg] *vt.* …의 호기심을 돋우다; *vi.* 음모를 꾸미다; *n.* 음모
If something intrigues you, it interests you and you want to know more about it.

astonish [əstániʃ] *vt.* 깜짝 놀라게 하다
To surprise greatly.

perplex [pərpléks] *vt.* 당황하게 하다, 당혹케 하다, 난처하게 하다
To confuse and worry someone slightly by being difficult to understand or solve.

mischief [místʃif] *n.* 장난; 해악
Behaviour which is slightly bad but is not intended to cause serious harm.

scrub [skrʌb] *v.* 북북 문지르다, 비벼서 씻다
To rub something hard in order to clean it.

for heaven's sake *idiom* 제발, 아무쪼록, 부디 (뒤에 오는 명령문을 강조함)
This is used in order to express annoyance or impatience, or to add force to a question or request.

fluster [flʌ́stər] *v.* 당황하다, 혼란스럽게 하다
If you fluster someone, you make them upset and confused.

provided [prəváidid] *conj.* …을 조건으로; 만약 …이면
If, or only if

swarm [swɔːrm] *vi.* 떼를 짓다; *n.* 떼, 무리
When people swarm somewhere, they move there in a large group.

track [træk] *v.* 추적하다, …의 뒤를 쫓다
To follow a person or animal by looking for proof that they have been somewhere, or by using electronic equipment.

pandemonium [pæ̀ndəmóuniəm] *n.* 수라장, 대혼란(의 곳)
A situation in which there is a lot of noise and confusion because people are excited, angry or frightened.

13. The Big Day Arrives

shield [ʃiːld] *v.* 보호하다, 지키다; *n.* 방패
To protect someone or something from being damaged.

bony [bóuni] *a.* 뼈의, 뼈뿐인
Very thin.

glimpse [glimps] *n.* 흘끗 보임, 일견
If you get a glimpse of something, you see them very briefly and not very well.

stencil [sténsil] *vt.* …에 스텐실[형판]을 대고 찍다, 등사하다
To draw or paint something using a stencil.

windbreaker [wíndbrèikər] *n.* (미) 스포츠용 재킷의 일종 (방풍 및 방한의 목적으로 손목과 허리 부분에 고무 밴드를 넣은 것)
A Windbreaker is a warm casual jacket.

fiend [fiːnd] *n.* 마귀, 악마(the Devil), 악령
An evil and cruel person.

dreadful [drédfəl] *a.* 무서운, 두려운, 무시무시한
Very bad, of very low quality, or shocking and very sad.

jeepers [dʒíːpərz] *int.* (미) 이런, 저런, 굉장하군 (놀람·열광의 표시)

creak [kriːk] *n.* 삐걱(거리는) 소리; *v.* 삐걱삐걱 하다[게 하다]
When a door or floorboard, etc. creaks, it makes a long low sound when it moves or is moved.

rusty [rʌ́sti] *a.* 녹슨
Covered with rust.

hinge [hindʒ] *n.* 돌쩌귀 (문짝을 문설주에 달아 여닫는 데 쓰는 두개의 쇠붙이)
A metal fastening that joins the edge of a door, window, lid, etc. to something else and allows it to swing open or closed.

14. Mr. Willy Wonka

plum [plʌm] *n.* 서양자두, 건포도 *a.* 건포도가 든, 짙은 자색의
A small round fruit with a thin smooth red, purple or yellow skin, sweet soft flesh, and a single large hard seed.

Build your Vocabulary

trouser [tráuzər] (= pants) *n.* 바지
A piece of clothing that you wear over your body from the waist downwards, and that cover each leg separately.

bottle green [bátlgri:n] *n.* 암녹색 (deep green)
Dark green in colour.

‡ **cane** [kein] *n.* 지팡이, 매, 회초리
A long stick used especially by old, ill or blind people to help them walk.

goatee [goutí:] *n.* (사람의 턱에 난) 염소수염
A small usually pointed beard grown only on the chin, not the cheeks.

J ★ **twinkle** [twíŋkəl] *v.* 반짝반짝 빛나다
To shine repeatedly strongly then weakly, as if flashing on and off very quickly.

jerky [dʒə́:rki] *a.* 갑자기 움직이는, 움찔하는, 실룩이는, 경련적인
Quick and sudden.

‡ **cock** [kák] *v.* 위로 치올리다, (귀·꽁지를) 쫑긋 세우다
To move a part of your body upwards or in a particular direction.

flutey [flu:ti] 플루트(flute) 소리 같은 (사전에 없는 단어. 저자가 만든 말)

M ‡ **seize** [si:z] *vt.* 붙잡다
To take hold of something quickly, firmly, and forcefully.

M **wart** [wɔ:rt] *n.* 사마귀
A small lump which grows on your skin.

enrapture [enrǽptʃər] *vt.* 황홀케 하다, 도취시키다
If something or someone enraptures you, you think they are wonderful or fascinating.

‡ **enchant** [intʃǽnt] *vt.* 매혹하다, 황홀하게 하다
To charm or please someone greatly.

★ **clang** [klæŋ] *n.* 쨍그렁, 뗑그렁 (소리); *v.* 뗑그렁 울리다
A loud ringing sound.

★ **trot** [trát] *v.* 속보로 걷다, 빨리 걷다; 총총걸음 치다
If you trot somewhere, you move fairly fast at a speed between walking and running, taking small quick step.

Chapter 11-15

J ‡ **perish** [périʃ] *v.* 멸망하다, 죽다, 썩어 없어지다; *n.* 궁핍 상태
To die, especially in an accident or by being killed, or to be destroyed.

‡ **corridor** [kɔ́:ridər] *n.* 복도
A long passage in a building or train, especially with rooms on either side.

★ **muffle** [mʌ́fəl] *vt.* (따뜻하게 하거나 감추기 위해) 싸다; 약하게[어둡게] 하다
To make something less strong or clear.

breakneck [bréiknèk] *a.* (목이 부러질 정도로) 위험 천만의; 몹시 가파른
Carelessly fast and dangerous.

M ‡ **peg** [peg] *n.* 나무 못, 쐐기, 걸이 못
A small stick or hook which sticks out from a surface and from which objects.

‡ **flap** [flæp] *v.* 펄럭이게 하다, 퍼덕이다; *n.* 펄럭임, 퍼덕거림; 혼란, 소동
To wave something, especially wings when or as if flying.

★ **shove** [ʃʌv] *v.* (난폭하게) 밀다, 밀치다; 밀어내다
To push someone or something forcefully.

★ **hustle** [hʌ́səl] *v.* 거칠게 밀치다, 떠밀다, 밀어 넣다, 밀어내다
To make someone move quickly by pushing or pulling them along.

‡ **bustle** [bʌ́səl] *vi.* 부산하게 움직이다, 붐비다, 재촉하다; *n.* 혼잡, 야단법석
To do things in a hurried and busy way.

dawdle [dɔ́:dl] *vt.* 빈둥거리다, 꾸물거리다; *vi.* (시간을) 부질없이 보내다
To do something or go somewhere very slowly, taking more time than is necessary.

warren [wɔ́(:)rən] *n.* 토끼 사육장; 많은 사람이 거주하는 건물
A series of connecting underground passages and holes in which rabbits live.

J ‡ **hollow** [hálou] *v.* 속이 비다[게 하다]; 도려내다, …을 파내어 만들다
Having a hole or empty space inside.

★ **downhill** [dáunhìl] *n.* 내리막길
Towards the bottom of a hill.

Build your Vocabulary

15. The Chocolate Room

abide [əbáid] *v.* 참다, 감수하다; 머무르다; 지속하다
If you can't abide someone or something, you dislike them very much

meadow [médou] *n.* 목초지, 풀밭
A field with grass and often wild flowers in it.

MJ 복습 **tremendous** [triméndəs] *a.* 거대한, 대단한; 엄청난, 무서운
Very great in amount or level, or extremely good.

churning [tʃə́:rniŋ] *n.* 우유 젓기; 1회 제조분의 버터
To mix something, especially a liquid, with great force.

whirlpool [hwə́:rlpù:l] *n.* 소용돌이
A small area of the sea or other water in which there is a powerful, circular current of water which can pull objects down into its centre.

MJ ★ **froth** [frɔ:θ] *n.* 거품 *v.* 거품을 일으키다
To have or produce a lot of small bubbles which often rise to the surface.

willow [wílou] *n.* 버드나무
A tree that grows near water and has long, thin branches that hang down.

★ **alder** [ɔ́:ldər] *n.* [식물] 오리나무속(屬)의 식물

J ★ **clump** [klʌmp] *n.* 수풀, (관목의) 덤불
A group, especially of trees or flowers.

rhododendron [ròudədéndrən] *n.* [식물] 철쭉속(屬)의 식물(만병초 따위)

mauve [mouv] *n.* 엷은 자주색; *a.* 엷은 자주색의
A pale purple colour.

buttercup [bʌ́tərkʌ̀p] *n.* [식물] 미나리아재비
A small, bright, yellow wild flower.

bathtub [bǽθtʌ̀b] *n.* (서양식) 욕조
A long container which is filled with water so that a person can sit or lie in it to wash their whole body.

J **flabbergast** [flǽbərgæ̀st] *vt.* (구어) 소스라쳐 놀라게 하다, 당황하게 하다
To shock someone, usually by telling them something they were not expecting.

Chapter 11-15

stagger [stǽgər] *v.* 비틀거리다[게 하다]; 흔들리다[게 하다]
To walk or move with a lack of balance as if you are going to fall.

dumfound [dʌmfáund] *vt.* …을 어이없어 말도 못하게 하다, 아연케 하다
If someone or something dumbfounds you, they surprise you very much.

bewilder [biwíldər] *vt.* 당황하게 하다, 어리둥절하게 하다
If something bewilders you, it is so confusing that you cannot understand it.

dazzle [dǽzəl] *vt.* 눈부시게 하다; 현혹시키다, 감탄시키다, 압도하다
If you are dazzled by someone or something, you think they are extremely good and exciting.

churn [tʃəːrn] *vt.* (물·흙 등을) 휘젓다, (통에 넣어 휘저어) 만들다
If something churns water, mud, or dust, it moves it about violently.

frothy [frɔ́ːθi] *a.* 거품투성이의, 거품 같은
A frothy liquid has lots of bubbles on its surface.

blade [bleid] *n.* 잎, 잎사귀 칼날
A blade of grass is a single piece of grass.

delectable [diléktəbəl] *a.* (종종 우스개) 즐거운, 기쁜, 유쾌한
If you describe something, especially food or drink, as delectable, you mean that it is very pleasant.

frantic [frǽntik] *a.* 광란의, 미친 듯 날뛰는 (frantically *ad.* 미친 듯이)
Behaving in a wild and uncontrolled way.

gosh [gaʃ] *int.* 아이쿠, 큰일났군 (God의 완곡한 말)
To be used to express surprise or strength of feeling.

Crossword Puzzle

Use the clues and the words in the box to complete the crossword puzzle.

corridor	sheer	peculiar	glimpse	envious	astonish	seize	trouser
stagger	blissful	verdict	dazzle	track	twinkle	cock	cluster
scrub	bony	flap	leap	mischief	perish	pupil	tremendous

Chapter 11-15

Across

4 A long passage in a building or train, especially with rooms on either side.
6 To follow a person or animal by looking for proof that they have been somewhere, or by using electronic equipment.
9 Used to emphasize how very great, important or powerful a quality or feeling is.
11 A piece of clothing that you wear over your body from the waist downwards, and that cover each leg separately.
14 The circular black area in the centre of your eye, through which light enters.
17 Extremely or completely happy.
19 To move a part of your body upwards or in a particular direction.
21 To walk or move with a lack of balance as if you are going to fall.
22 To die, especially in an accident or by being killed, or to be destroyed.
23 To take hold of something quickly, firmly, and forcefully.
24 To wave something, especially wings when or as if flying.

Down

1 Unusual and strange, sometimes in an unpleasant way.
2 Very great in amount or level, or extremely good.
3 An opinion or decision made after judging the facts that are given, especially one made at the end of a tial.
5 If you are _____ d by someone or something, you think they are extremely good and exciting.
7 To surprise greatly.
8 Very thin.
10 If you are _____ of someone, you want something that they have.
12 To rub something hard in order to clean it.
13 To see something very briefly and not very well.
15 To shine repeatedly strongly then weakly, as if flashing on and off very quickly.
16 If people _____ together, they gather together in a small group.
18 Behaviour which is slightly bad but is not intended to cause serious harm.
20 To make a large jump or sudden movement, usually from one place to another.

Comprehension Quiz

1. Which one is not a dangerous beast from Loompa land?

A. Snozzwangers

B. Whangdoodles

C. Rotten vermiscious kenids

D. Hornswogglers

2. Which is the food that the Oompa-Loompas didn't eat?

A. Green caterpillars

B. Red beetles

C. Eucalyptus leaves

D. Raspberries

Chapter 16 **The Oompa-Loompas**

3. How did Wonka convince the Oompa-Loompas to come to his factory?

A. He said they could earn a lot of money

B. He said they could eat cacao beans and chocolate every day

C. He said they would be safe from the dangerous creatures

D. He said they would work hard all day in a factory

4. How did Wonka get the Oompa-Loompas to his factory?

(A)_____

5. What are the Oompa-Loompas like? (two answers)

A. They wear deer skins or leaves

B. They like to sing and dance

C. They don't speak English

D. They are lazy and do not work hard

Comprehension Quiz

1. Why is Wonka worried when Augustus is scooping up the hot melted chocolate?
A. Because Augustus will fall into the river
B. Because Augustus will make the chocolate dirty
C. Because the melted chocolate isn't delicious
D. Because the amount of the melted chocolate is too small

2. Who did Augustus listen to?
A. Mr. Wonka
B. His mother
C. His stomach
D. His father

Chapter 17 **Augustus Gloop Goes up the Pipe**

3. Why didn't Mr. Gloop dive in to save his son?

A. Mr. Gloop does not like chocolate

B. He cannot swim

C. He does not want his best suit to get dirty

D. He wants to see his son go up the pipe

4. Mrs. Gloop says that Augustus will be made into marshmallows, but Mr. Wonka says that is impossible. Why?

A. Because that pipe does not go to the marshmallow room

B. Because Augustus is too big to be not made into marshmallows

C. Because that pipe go to the inventing room

D. Because Mr. Wonka will rescue him from that pipe

5. What was Mr. Wonka doing while Mr. and Mrs. Gloop were so worried about their son?

A. He was joking and giggling

B. He began hopping and dancing and beating small drums

C. He worried about Augustus so much

D. He ordered Oompa-Loompas to rescue their son

Comprehension Quiz

1. What did the pink boat look like?

A. A Viking boat

B. A boiled sweet

C. A pirate ship

D. A chocolate boat

2. What is the most astonishing thing Charlie has seen so far?

A. The waterfall

B. The sucking pipes

C. Mr. Wonka

D. The pink boat

3. Why did Wonka give Charlie and Grandpa Joe mugs of chocolate?

A. Because they seem like chocolate so much

B. Because they were too skinny

C. Because they like melted chocolate more than bars

D. Because Mr.Wonka wanted to boast about his chocolate

4. Which cream is different from the others?

A. Whipped cream

B. Coffee cream

C. Vanilla cream

D. Hair cream

Chapter 18 **Down the Chocolate River**

5. What are the whips in storeroom 71 used for?

A. Beating the naughty Oompa-Loompas

B. Working in the Oompa-Loompa circus

C. Whipping the whipped cream

D. Swinging in the trees

Comprehension Quiz

1. Who is Mr. Wonka inventing Gobstoppers for?

A. Children who like all of Wonka's chocolates

B. Children who seem too skinny

C. Children who are sincere

D. Children with very little pocket money

2. What do Gobstoppers look like?

A. A flat small box

B. A marble

C. A small die

D. An erase

3. What is special about Gobstoppers?

A. They change shapes

B. You can make giant bubbles

C. They never get smaller

D. They taste like frogs

Chapter 19 **The Inventing Room-Everlasting Gobstoppers and Hair Toffee**

4. What happens when you eat Hair Toffee?

A. In 30 minutes, you become a chocolate river

B. In 30 minutes, you float on the ceiling

C. In 30 minutes, you become smaller than an inch tall

D. In 30 minutes, you grow hair on your head, a moustache, and a beard

5. After eating Hair Toffee, what did they have to do?

A. They didn't have to do anything

B. They had to use a lawn mower to keep it in check

C. They had to take an antidote

D. They had to get a hair cut with scissors

Comprehension Quiz

1. What does not the gum machine do?

A. The machine shakes

B. Hisses out steam

C. Jumps up and down

D. Squirts runny stuff into a tub

2. What sounds does not the gum machine make?

A. Mighty groaning

B. Screaming

C. Whizzing

D. Rumbling

3. Why is Mike Teavee disappointed?

A. The big noisy machine only makes a little stick of gum

B. A new gum taste bitter

C. He likes only chocolates

D. He lose interest in the chocolate factory

Chapter 20 **The Great Gum Machine**

4. Why is Violet so excited?

A. She loves the unique machine

B. She loves gum

C. The machine has a miraculous power

D. A new gum has a special shape

Build your Vocabulary

16. The Oompa-Loompas

* **infest** [infést] *vt.* (해충 · 도둑 등이) …에 횡행하다; 만연하다, 몰려들다
  When creatures such as insects or rats infest plants or a place, they are present in large numbers and cause damage.

  hornswoggle 로알드 달이 자신의 작품 속에 창조한 생물. 번역서에는 '뿔 쌩쌩이'라고 번역되어 있다.

  snozzwanger 로알드 달이 자신의 작품 속에 창조한 생물. 번역서에는 '킁킁왕왕이'라고 번역되어 있다.

  whangdoodle 로알드 달이 자신의 작품 속에 창조한 생물. 번역서에는 '왕 알알이'라고 번역되어 있다.

* **caterpillar** [kǽtərpìlər] *n.* 모충(毛蟲), 풀쐐기(나비 · 나방 따위의 유충)

* **revolt** [rivóult] *v.* 비위가 상하다[게 하다]; 반항[배반]하다; *n.* 반란, 폭동
  To make someone feel unpleasantly shocked or disgusted.

  mash up *idiom* 충분히 으깨다
  To crush something, especially food.

  eucalyptus [jùːkəlíptəs] *n.* [식물] 유칼립투스(오스트레일리아 원산의 교목)

* **crave** [kreiv] *v.* 열망하다, 갈망하다, 간절히 원하다
  A strong or uncontrollable desire.

  dribble [dríbəl] *v.* 공을 드리블하다; (물방울 등이) 똑똑 떨어지다
  To keep tapping a ball quickly in order to keep it moving.

* **gorge** [gɔːrdʒ] *v.* 배불리 먹다, 포식하다
  To eat until you are unable to eat any more.

* **smuggle** [smʌ́gəl] *v.* 밀수입하다, 몰래 들여오다
  To take things or people to or from a place secretly and often illegally.

* **mischievous** [místʃivəs] *a.* 장난이 심한, 개구쟁이의; 유해한, 화를 미치는
  A mischievous person likes to have fun by playing harmless tricks on people or doing things they are not supposed to do.

* **sneak** [sniːk] *v.* 몰래[살금살금] 움직이다
  If you sneak somewhere, you go there very quietly on foot, trying to avoid being seen.

Chapter 16-20

17. Augustus Gloop Goes up the Pipe

waggle [wǽgəl] *v.* 흔들다, 흔들리다
To move quickly up and down or from side to side.

lap [læp] *n.* 한 바퀴; 무릎
A single journey around a race track.

shriek [ʃriːk] *n.* 날카로운 소리, 비명; *v.* 새된 소리로 말하다
A short, loud, high cry.

drown [draun] *v.* 잠기다, 익사하다
If a loud noise drowns out another noise, it prevents it from being heard.

wretched [rétʃid] *a.* 비참한, 불쌍한; 초라한; 야비한, 비열한
Unhappy, unpleasant or of low quality.

dangle [dǽŋgəl] *v.* 매달다[리다]; 따라다니다; *n.* 매달린 것
To hang loosely, or to hold something so that it hangs loosely.

torpedo [tɔːrpíːdou] *n.* 어뢰, 공중 어뢰; *v.* 어뢰로 파괴하다
The Bomb shaped like a tube and that travels under water.

murder [mə́ːrdər] *n.* 살인, 살인 사건
The deliberate and illegal killing of a person.

smash [smæʃ] *v.* 분쇄하다, 박살내다
To break something into many pieces.

swish [swiʃ] *v.* 휙 소리내다; 휘두르다; *n.* 휙휙(날개·채찍 따위의 소리)
To move quickly through the air making a soft sound.

blockage [blάkidʒ] *n.* 봉쇄; 방해; 방해물, 차단물
Something that stops something else passing through, or when something does this.

brigade [brigéid] *n.* (군대식 편성의) 대(隊), 조(組) (fire brigade : 소방대)
A large group of soldiers in an army.

marshmallow [mάːrʃmèlou] *n.* 마시멜로 (녹말·시럽 등으로 만드는 과자)
A soft sweet pink or white food.

inconceivable [ìnkənsíːvəbəl] *a.* 상상할 수 없는; (구어) 믿을 수 없는
Impossible to imagine or think of.

Build your Vocabulary

- **absurd** [əbsə́:rd] *a.* 불합리한, 부조리한, 터무니없는
  ridiculous or unreasonable; foolish in an amusing way.

- **indignant** [indígnənt] *a.* 분개한, 성난 (indignantly *ad.* 분개하여)
  Feeling or showing anger.

- **sling** [sliŋ] *vt.* 던져 올리다, 걸치다; 투석기로 쏘다, 내던지다; *n.* 투석기
  To hang something over something, especially in a careless way.

- **explode** [iksplóud] *v.* 폭발하다
  If an object such as a bomb explodes, it bursts loudly and with great force.

- **peal** [pi:l] *n.* 울림
  A long loud sound or series of sounds, especially of laughter or thunder.

- **fury** [fjúəri] *n.* 격노, 격분; 격정, 열광, 맹렬함
  Extreme anger.

- **chant** [tʃænt] *v.* (노래를) 부르다; 일제히 외치다
  To sing a religious prayer or song to a simple tune.

- **nincompoop** [nínkəmpù:p] *n.* 바보, 멍청이
  A foolish or stupid person

- **guzzle** [gʌ́zəl] *v.* 폭음하다, 꿀꺽꿀꺽 마시다, 게걸스럽게 먹다
  To eat or drink quickly, eagerly and usually in large amounts.

- **feast** [fi:st] *n.* 축제, 축연, 진수성찬; *v.* 축연을 베풀다, 진수성찬을 먹다
  A day on which a religious event or person is remembered and celebrated.

- **brat** [bræt] *n.* (경멸적) 선머슴, 개구쟁이
  A child, especially one who behaves badly.

- **unutterable** [ʌ̀nʌ́tərəbəl] *a.* 말로 표현할 수 없는; 철저한, 순전한
  Too bad to be expressed in words.

- **vile** [vail] *a.* 비열한, 야비한
  Unpleasant, immoral and unacceptable.

- **alter** [ɔ́:ltər] *v.* 변하다, 바꾸다, 변경하다, 고치다
  To change something, usually slightly, or to cause the characteristics of something to change.

Chapter 16-20

cog [kɔ́g] *n.* (톱니바퀴의) 이
One of the tooth-like parts around the edge of a wheel in a machine which fits between those of a similar wheel, causing both wheels to move.

grind [graind] *vt.* 타다, 갈다; 가루로 만들다, 으깨다
To make something into small pieces or a powder by pressing between hard surfaces.

spice [spais] *n.* 양념, 향신료, 양념류; *vt.* …에 양념을 치다
A substance made from a plant, which is used to give a special flavour to food.

gall [gɔːl] *n.* 쓸개즙, 쓴 것[맛]; 불쾌, 지겨움, 뻔뻔스러움
Rudeness and inability to understand that your behaviour or what you say is not acceptable to other people.

loathe [louθ] *vt.* 몹시 싫어하다, 진저리를 내다, 질색하다
To be unwilling to do something.

brute [bruːt] *n.* 짐승, 야만인; *a.* 잔인한, 야만적인, 무정한
A rough and sometimes violent man.

louse [laus] *n.* [곤충] 이; 기생충; (구어) 비열한 놈, 인간쓰레기

grudge [grʌdʒ] *vt.* 주기 싫어하다, 인색하게 굴다, 못마땅해 하다; *n.* 악의, 원한
A strong feeling of anger and dislike for a person who you feel has treated you badly, which often lasts for a long time.

luscious [lʌ́ʃəs] *a.* 감미로운, 달콤한
Having a pleasant sweet taste or containing a lot of juice.

18. Down the Chocolate River

be bound to *idiom* 반드시 …하다, 하게 마련이다
If you say that something is bound to happen or be true, you feel confident and certain of it.

mist [mist] *n.* 안개; *v.* 안개가 끼다, 눈이 흐려지다
Thin fog produced by very small drops of water gathering in the air just above an area of ground or water.

glisten [glisn] *vi.* 반짝이다, 빛나다
If something glistens, it shines, usually because it is wet or oily.

Build your Vocabulary

- **oar** [ɔːr] *n.* 노
  A long pole with a wide, flat end that you use to move a boat through water.

- **hollow** [hálou] *v.* 속이 비다[게 하다]; 도려내다, …을 파내어 만들다
  Having a hole or empty space inside.

- **gleam** [gliːm] *n.* 어스레한 빛; 번득[번쩍]임; *vi.* 어슴푸레 빛나다; 번득이다
  To produce or reflect a small, bright light.

- **colossal** [kəlásəl] *a.* 거대한, (구어) 어마어마한, 굉장한
  If you describe something as colossal, you are emphasizing that it is very large.

- **lick** [lik] *vt.* 핥다; 스치다, 넘실거리다
  To move the tongue across the surface of something.

- **kick in** *phrasal verb* 시동하다, 움직이기 시작하다
  If something kicks in, it begins to take effect.

- **astonish** [əstániʃ] *vt.* 깜짝 놀라게 하다
  To surprise greatly.

- **marvellous** [máːrvələs] (= marvelous) *a.* 놀라운, 믿기 어려운; (구어) 훌륭한
  Extremely good.

- **grin** [grin] *v.* 이를 드러내고 싱긋 웃다; 이를 악물다[드러내다]
  A wide smile.

- **tummy** [támi] *n.* (유아어) 배 (stomach)
  Your tummy is the part of the front of your body below your waist.

- **tingle** [tíŋgəl] *n.* 따끔거림, 쑤심; 흥분; *v.* 따끔따끔 아프다, 쑤시다; 설레다
  If you tingle with a feeling such as excitement, you feel it very strongly.

- **intense** [inténs] *a.* 강렬한, 심한
  Extreme in degree, strength, or size.

- **smack** [smæk] *vt.* 찰싹 치다; *n.* 찰싹 하는 소리
  To hit something hard against something else so that it makes a short loud noise.

- **pitch dark** [pítʃdáːrk] *a.* 캄캄한, 칠흑 같은
  Extremely dark.

Chapter 16-20

- ★ **hoot** [huːt] *vi.* 야유하다; (올빼미가) 부엉부엉 울다; *n.* 부엉부엉 (올빼미 울음소리)
  The sound an owl makes.

- ★ **speck** [spek] *n.* 작은 반점, 얼룩; 작은 조각, 단편; 적은 양, 소량
  A very small mark, piece or amount.

- **aghast** [əgǽst] *a.* 소스라치게, 놀라서, 겁이 나서
  Suddenly filled with strong feelings of shock and anxiety.

- ★ **balmy** [báːmi] *a.* (속어) 얼빠진, 얼간이의
  Slightly crazy.

- **nutty** [nʌ́ti] *a.* (속어) 머리가 돈, 미치광이
  Crazy, foolish or strange.

- **screwy** [skrúːi] *a.* (속어) 인색한, 정신 나간, 어딘가 별난, 매우 이상한
  Very strange, foolish or unusual.

- **batty** [bǽti] *a.* (구어) 머리가 돈(crazy); 어리석은(silly)
  Silly and foolish with confused behaviour.

- **dippy** [dipi] *a.* (속어) 미친, 환장한, 엉뚱한, 터무니없는
  Silly.

- **dotty** [dɔ́ti] *a.* 점이 많은; (구어) 머리가 돈; 휘청대는, 흔들리는
  Slightly strange or mentally ill.

- **daffy** [dǽfi] *a.* (구어) 어리석은; 미친
  strange or unusual, sometimes in an amusing way.

- **goofy** [gúːfi] *a.* (속어) 얼빠진, 어리석은, 제정신이 아닌
  Silly.

- **beany** [bíːni] *a.* (속어) 기운찬; 기분이 좋은; 정신이 이상한

- ★ **buggy** [bʌ́gi] ① *n.* 2륜 경마차 ② *a.* (속어) 미친, 열중하고 있는; 벌레투성이의

- **wacky** [wǽki] *a.* (속어) 괴짜인, 이상한, 괴팍스러운, 엉뚱한
  Unusual in a pleasing and exciting or silly way.

- **loony** [lúːni] *a.* (구어) 미친, 머리가 돈(crazy); 바보 같은, 어리석은
  Foolish or stupid.

Build your Vocabulary

‡ furious [fjúəriəs] *a.* 성난, 격노한; 맹렬한, 왕성한 (furiously *ad.* 맹렬하게)
Extremely angry; Using a lot of effort or strength.

★ **whiz** [hwiz] *n.* (속어) 명수, 명인; 윙, 씽, 핑(공중을 가르는 소리)

‡ **streak** [stri:k] *v.* 줄무늬지다; 질주하다; *n.* 줄, 선
To move somewhere extremely quickly, usually in a straight line.

‡ **whip** [hwip] *v.* 채찍질하다; 급히 움직이다
If someone whips something out, they take it out very quickly and suddenly.

poach [poutʃ] *vt.* 데치다, (깬 달걀을) 흩뜨리지 않고 뜨거운 물에 삶다
(a poached egg : 깨어 삶은 달걀)
To cook something such as a fish, or an egg with its shell removed, by putting it in gently boiling water or other liquid.

19. The Inventing Room-Everlasting Gobstoppers and Hair Toffee

★ **alongside** [əlɔ́:ŋsàid] *ad., prep.* …에 옆으로 대고
Beside, or together with.

★ **simmer** [símər] *vi.* 부글부글 끓다, 약한 불로 끓이다
To cook something liquid, or something with liquid in it, at a temperature slightly below boiling.

‡ **meddle** [médl] *vi.* 쓸데없이 참견하다, 간섭하다
To try to change or have an influence on things which are not your responsibility, especially in a critical, damaging or annoying way.

‡ **scramble** [skrǽmbəl] *vi.* 급히 움직이다
If you scramble to a different place, you move there in a hurried.

‡ **kettle** [kétl] *n.* 솥, 주전자

★ **hiss** [his] *n.* 쉿 소리; 쉿 하는 소리를 내다
To make a long noise like the letter 's'.

sizzle [sízəl] *v.* (튀김이나 고기 구울 때) 지글거리다, 지글지글 소리가 나게 굽다
To make a sound like food cooking in hot fat.

Chapter 16-20

clank [klæŋk] *v.* (무거운 쇠붙이 등이) 절거덕 하고 소리 나다[게 하다]
To make a short loud sound like that of metal objects hitting each other, or to cause something to make this sound.

복습 **splutter** [splʌ́tər] (= sputter) *vi.* 푸푸 소리를 내다; 입에서 침을 튀기다
To works or burns in an uneven way and makes a series of soft popping sounds.

★ **saucepan** [sɔ́:spæ̀n] *n.* (자루·뚜껑이 달린) 스튜 냄비
A deep round pan with straight sides, usually with a handle and a lid.

★ **lid** [lid] *n.* 뚜껑
A cover on a container, which can be removed.

★ **knob** [náb] *n.* 손잡이, 쥐는 곳; 혹, 마디; (깃대 따위의) 둥근 장식
A round handle, or a small round device for controlling a machine or electrical equipment.

복습 **peer** [piər] *vi.* 자세히 보다, 응시하다
To look at something very hard.

J ★ **marble** [má:rbəl] *n.* 구슬; 대리석; (pl.) (속어) 정상의 판단력, 분별
A small ball usually made of coloured or transparent glass which is used in children's games.

★ **everlasting** [èvərlǽstiŋ] *a.* 영원히 계속되는; 끝없는, 지루한
Lasting forever or for a long time.

gobstopper [gábstápər] *n.* (영) 크고 둥근 딱딱한 캔디
A large round hard sweet which often has different coloured layers.

toffee [tɔ́:fi] *n.* 태피(taffy) (설탕, 버터 따위로 만든 과자)
A hard, chewy, often brown sweet that is made from sugar boiled with butter.

복습 **gooey** [gú:i] *a.* 끈적끈적한, 들러붙는; *n.* 끈적거리는 것, 당밀
Soft and sticky.

purplish [pə́:rpliʃ] *a.* 자줏빛을 띤
Almost purple in colour.

treacle [trí:kəl] *n.* (영) 당밀; *a.* 달콤한, 당밀 같은
A sweet dark thick liquid which is used in cooking sweet dishes and sweets.

Build your Vocabulary

luscious [lʌ́ʃəs] *a.* 감미로운, 달콤한
Having a pleasant sweet taste or containing a lot of juice.

crop [kráp] *n.* 수확, 농작물, 곡물
A plant such as a grain, fruit or vegetable grown in large amounts.

moustache [mʌ́stæʃ] (= mustache) *n.* (미) 코밑수염 ;동물의 수염
Hair which a man grows above his upper lip.

for heaven's sake *idiom* 제발, 아무쪼록
Used in order to express annoyance or impatience, or to add force to a question or request.

20. The Great Gum Machine

gleam [gli:m] *n.* 어스레한 빛; 번득[번쩍]임; *vi.* 어슴푸레 빛나다; 번득이다
To produce or reflect a small, bright light.

sprout [spraut] *vi.* 싹이 트다, 발아하다
To start to grow, producing shoots, buds, or leaves.

tub [tʌb] (=bathtub) *n.* 통, 물통, 욕조, 목욕통
A bathtub is a long, usually rectangular container which you fill with water and sit in to wash your body.

mighty [máiti] *a.* 강력한, 힘센, 중대한; 굉장한, 대단한
Very large, powerful or important.

rumble [rʌ́mbəl] *n.* 우르르 울리는 소리; *v.* 우르르 울리다
A low continuous noise.

squirt [skwə:rt] *v.* 분출하다[시키다], 뿜어[대다]
to flow out through a narrow opening in a fast stream

runny [rʌ́ni] *a.* 흐르는 경향이 있는, 액체 비슷한, 점액을 잘 분비하는
Something that is runny is more liquid than usual or than was intended.

slosh [sláʃ] *n.* (액체가) 튀어 흩어짐, 튀어 오름; *v.* 절벅절벅 휘젓다, 물을 튀기다
to move around noisily in the bottom of a container, or to cause liquid to move around in this way by making rough movements

whiz [hwiz] *n.* (속어) 명수, 명인; 웡, 씽, 핑(공중을 가르는 소리)

Chapter 16-20

MJ ★ **froth** [frɔ́:θ] *n.* 거품 *v.* 거품을 일으키다
To have or produce a lot of small bubbles which often rise to the surface.

‡ **queer** [kwiər] *a.* 기묘한, 괴상한; 수상한; (속어) 동성애의
Strange, unusual or not expected

★ **monstrous** [mάnstrəs] *a.* 괴물 같은, 기괴한; 거대한
Very bad or cruel.

‡ **groan** [groun] *v.* 신음하다, 끙끙거리다
To make a long deep sound because you are in pain, upset, or disappointed.

‡ **drawer** [drɔ́:ər] *n.* 서랍
A box-shaped container without a top which is part of a piece of furniture. It slides in and out to open and close and is used for keeping things in.

strip [strip] *n.* 길고 가느다란 조각
A long flat narrow piece.

복습 **goofy** [gú:fi] *a.* (속어) 얼빠진, 어리석은, 제정신이 아닌
Silly.

‡ **slap** [slæp] *v.* 찰싹 때리다, 털썩 놓다
To hit someone with the flat part of the hand or other flat object.

MJ ★ **fabulous** [fǽbjələs] *a.* 굉장한, 멋진; 믿어지지 않는, 전설적인
Very good; excellent.

Crossword Puzzle

Use the clues and the words in the box to complete the crossword puzzle.

wretched	grind	whiz	crave	simmer	hollow	sneack	scramble
fabulous	grin	lick	grudge	gorge	chant	revolt	lid
luscious	gleam	feast	peer	shriek	dangle	dribble	meddle
groan	inconceivable						

Chapter 16-20

Across

1. Unhappy, unpleasant or of low quality.
3. To sing a religious prayer or song to a simple tune.
5. To make something into small pieces or a powder by pressing between hard surfaces.
6. To cook something liquid, or something with liquid in it, at a temperature slightly below boiling.
8. To eat until you are unable to eat any more.
12. A wide smile.
13. To try to change or have an influence on things which are not your responsibility, especially in a critical, damaging or annoying way.
15. Having a hole or empty space inside.
16. To move the tongue across the surface of something.
17. A strong feeling of anger and dislike for a person who you feel has treated you badly, which often lasts for a long time.
18. To keep tapping it quickly in order to keep it moving.
19. A day on which a religious event or person is remembered and celebrated.
20. If you _____ to a different place, you move there in a hurried.
22. To make someone feel unpleasantly shocked or disgusted.
23. To go somewhere very quietly on foot, trying to avoid being seen.
24. _____ kid : a wonder child.

Down

2. A strong or uncontrollable desire.
4. To make a long deep sound because you are in pain, upset, or disappointed.
5. To produce or reflect a small, bright light.
7. Impossible to imagine or think of.
9. A cover on a container, which can be removed.
10. To look at something very hard.
11. A short, loud, high cry.
14. To hang loosely, or to hold something so that it hangs loosely.
19. Very good; excellent.
21. Having a pleasant sweet taste or containing a lot of juice.

Comprehension Quiz

1. What are not the benefits of the chewing gum meal?

A. No cooking

B. No garbage

C. No eating

D. No washing the dishes

2. What is not on the menu for this chewing gum meal?

A. Tomato soup

B. Roast beef

C. Chocolate bar

D. Blueberry pie

3. Why does Mr. Wonka tell Violet to stop?

A. Because Mr. Wonka didn't want to give gum to anybody

B. Because Mr. Wonka was worried about some harmful ingredients in the gum

C. Because the gum is too hard to chew

D. Because the gum is not perfected yet

4. Why doesn't Violet listen to Mr. Wonka? (two answers)

A. She loves gum

B. She is hungry

C. She is stubborn

D. She is chewing gum

Chapter 21 **Good-bye Violet**

5. What does not happen to Violet?

A. She blows up like ballon

B. She fills with gum

C. Her nose and cheeks turn purple

D. She is taken to the juicing room

Comprehension Quiz

1. Which is not a name of a door that Mr. Wonka and others walk past?

A. Marshmallow pillows

B. Lickable wallpaper for nurseries

C. Hot ice creams for cold days

D. Cotton candy sheep

2. What fruit is not on Lickable Wallpaper? (two answers)

A. Snozzberry

B. Banana

C. Jackfruit

D. Durian

3. If you drink Fizzy Lifting Drinks how do you get down?

A. You have to burp

B. You have to go to the bathroom

C. You have to throw them up

D. You have to eat nothing for a night

Chapter 22 **Along the Corridor**

4. What if you drink Fizzy Lifting Drinks outside and do not burp?
A. You will swell up
B. You will go to the moon
C. Nothing happens
D. You will fly to another country

5. Why do they pass by so many interesting rooms without stopping?
A. Because there are too many interesting rooms to stop and see all of them
B. Because the rooms do not really have anything inside
C. Because Wonka does not want to give away his most precious candy making secrets
D. Because Wonka lost his keys and cannot open the doors

Comprehension Quiz

1. What shape are the candies?

A. ○   B. □   C. ◇   D. △

2. What can the candies do?

A. Drink Buttergin

B. Sing with the Oompa-Loompas

C. Dance with Mr. Wonka

D. Move their faces

3. What drinks do the Oompa-Loompas like best of all?

A. Butterscotch and soda

B. Scotch and soda

C. Scotch and Gin

D. Gin and tonic

Chapter 23 **Square Candies That Look Round**

4. What does 'tiddly' mean?

(A)_____

5. What does "Mrs. Salt was blowing like a rhinoceros" mean? (two answers)

A. She was out of breath

B. She was making balloons

C. She was tired

D. She was having a birthday party

Comprehension Quiz

1. What does Mr. Wonka use to get the nuts out of the shells?

(A)_____

2. Why do the squirrels tap the walnuts with their knuckles before opening them?

(A)_____

Chapter 24 **Veruca in th Nut Room**

3. Where do the squirrels throw the bad nuts?
A. Into the glass pipes

B. Into the inventing room

C. Into the gum machine

D. Down the garbage chute

4. Who did rush in the Nut Room?
A. Charlie

B. Mr. Wonka

C. Veruca

D. Teavee

5. How often does the incinerator work?
A. Once a day

B. Every other day

C. Every othe Week

D. Every Monday

Comprehension Quiz

1. Which direction can the elevator go?
(A)_____
(B)_____
(C)_____
(D)_____

2. How many buttons are there in the elevator?
A. 500   B. 1000   C. 3000   D. 5000

3. Name your four favorite elevator buttons.
(A)_____
(B)_____
(C)_____
(D)_____

4. What did Mr. Wonka and others not see from the elevator?
A. A giant fudge mountain

B. An Oompa-Loompa village

C. A lake of hot caramel

D. Another elevator

Chapter 25 **The Great Glass Elevator**

5. Why is Mrs. Teavee going to be sick?

A. Because she thinks that the elevator will fly

B. Because the elevator is like a roller coaster

C. Because Wonka says that there is another elevator on the same track

D. Because she does not like elevators

Build your Vocabulary

21. Good-by Violet

utter [ʌ́tər] ① *a.* 완전한, 전적인 ② *v.* (소리·말 등을) 입 밖에 내다, 발언하다
Complete or extreme.

MJ **obstinate** [ábstənit] *a.* 완고한, 고집 센
Unreasonably determined, especially to act in a particular way and not to change at all, despite argument or persuasion.

복습 **heck** [hek] *n.* 지옥(hell의 완곡한 말)
Used to say that you will do something although you know you should not do it.

tongs [tɔ(ː)ŋz] *n.* (단·복수취급) (a pair of…) 집게; 부젓가락
A device used for picking up objects, consisting of two long pieces joined at one end and pressed together at the other end in order to hold an object between them.

spit [spit] *v.* 뱉다, 토해내다, 뿜어내다
To force out the contents of the mouth, especially saliva.

MJ **spellbound** [spélbàund] *a.* 마법에 걸린, 넋을 잃은
Having your attention completely held by something, so that you cannot think about anything else.

rubbery [rʌ́bəri] *a.* 고무 같은, 탄력(성) 있는, 질긴
Feeling or bending like rubber.

J **wring** [riŋ] *v.* 짜다, 비틀다; 몸부림치다
To hold something tightly with both hands and twist it by turning your hands in opposite directions.

MJ **peculiar** [pikjúːljər] *a.* 기묘한, 이상한; 특이한, 눈에 띄는
Unusual and strange, sometimes in an unpleasant way.

mop [máp] *v.* 자루걸레로 닦다; *n.* 자루걸레
If you mop a floor, you clean it with a mop.

swell [swel] *v.* 부풀다[부풀게 하다], 붓다, 팽창하다 (up, out); 증가하다[시키다]
To become larger and rounder than usual.

J **screech** [skriːtʃ] *vi.* 새된 소리를 내다, 비명을 지르다; *n.* 날카로운 소리, 비명
To make a unpleasant loud high noise.

Chapter 21-25

* **prick** [prik] *v.* (바늘 따위로) 찌르다, 쑤시다; *n.* 찌름, 쑤심
  To make a very small hole or holes in the surface of something.

J 음 **repulsive** [ripʌ́lsiv] *a.* 되쫓아버리는, 박차는; 쌀쌀한, 싫은, 불쾌한
  Extremely unpleasant or unacceptable.

bum [bʌm] *n.* 부랑자, 게으름뱅이
  Someone who has no home or job and lives by asking other people for money.

* **ludicrous** [lúːdəkrəs] *a.* 익살맞은, 우스운, 바보 같은
  Stupid or unreasonable and deserving to be laughed at.

* **linoleum** [linóuliəm] 리놀륨(마루의 깔개)
  A stiff smooth material that is used for covering floors.

J * **horrid** [hɔ́ːrid] *a.* 무시무시한; 매우 불쾌한, 지겨운
  Unpleasant or unkind.

J * **groove** [gruːv] *n.* 홈, 바퀴 자국; 관례, 습관
  A long narrow hollow space cut into a surface.

* **dumb** [dʌm] *a.* 벙어리의, 말을 못하는, 말을 하지 않는
  Permanently or temporarily unable to speak.

* **sanatorium** [sæ̀nətɔ́ːriəm] *n.* 새너토리엄, (특히 정신병·결핵 환자의) 요양소
  A special type of hospital, usually in the countryside, where people can have treatment and rest, especially when getting better after a long illness.

22. Along the Corridor

* **naughty** [nɔ́ːti] *a.* 장난꾸러기인, 행실이 나쁜
  When children are naughty, they behave badly or are not obedient

de-juice [di-dʒuːs] juice(즙)을 제거하다 (저자가 만든 단어)

* **whistle** [hwísəl] *n.* 휘파람, 호각; *vi.* 휘파람 불다, 휘파람으로 부르다
  If something whistles somewhere, it moves there, making a loud, high sound.

MJ * **mumble** [mʌ́mbəl] *v.* 중얼거리다; 우물우물 씹다; *n.* 중얼거림
  To speak unclearly and quietly so that the words are difficult to understand.

Build your Vocabulary

scuttle [skʌ́tl] *vi.* 급히 가다, 황급히 달리다; 허둥지둥 도망가다; *n.* 종종걸음
To move quickly, with small short steps, especially in order to escape.

mess [mes] *n.* 난잡, 혼란, 엉망진창
An untidy or dirty state.

perch [pəːrtʃ] *v.* 앉다, 자리를 차지하다, (높은 곳에) 놓다, 앉히다
To sit on or near the edge of something.

coattail [kóuttèil] *n.* (흔히 pl.) (야회복, 모닝 등의) 상의의 뒷자락

waft [wáːft] *v.* 둥둥 떠돌다, (냄새 따위가) 풍기다
To (cause to) move gently through the air.

lickable 핥을 수 있는 (저자가 조합한 단어, lick *v.* 핥다, able *a.* … 할 수 있는)

nursery [nə́ːrsəri] *n.* 육아실, 탁아소, 보육원; 양성소, 훈련소
A place where young children and babies are taken care of while their parents are at work.

snozzberry 로알드 달이 자신의 작품 속에 만들어낸 과일 이름. 번역서에는 '킁킁딸기'로 번역되어 있다.

fizzy [fizi] *a.* 쉬잇 하고 거품이 이는, 청량감이 드는
Having a lot of bubbles; You can use it when something is strangely good, with a bubbling sensation.

terrific [tərífik] *a.* 굉장한, 엄청난; 무서운, 소름이 끼치는
(terrifically *ad.* 굉장히, 지독히, 몹시)
Very good; excellent.

burp [bəːrp] *n., v.* 트림(이 나다); (갓난아이에게 젖을 먹인 후) 트림을 시키다
To allow air from the stomach to come out through the mouth in a noisy way.

skid [skid] *v.* 미끄러지다; *n.* (무거운 물건을 굴릴 때 까는) 활재, 굴대; 미끄럼
To slide along a surface so that you have no control.

peek [piːk] *v.* 살짝 들여다보다, 엿보다
If you peek at something, you have a quick look at them.

23. Square Candies That Look Round

lump [lʌmp] *n.* 덩어리, 한 조각; (구어) 땅딸보; 멍청이, 바보
A piece of a solid substance, usually with no particular shape.

fling [fliŋ] (flung–flung) *vt.* 던지다, 내던지다
To throw something somewhere using a lot of force.

row [rou] *n.* 열, 줄; 좌석 줄
A line of things, people, animals, etc. arranged next to each other.

triumphant [traiʌ́mfənt] *a.* 승리를 한, 의기양양한
(triumphantly *ad.* 의기양양하게)
Having achieved a great victory or success.

golly [gáli] *int.* 저런, 어머나, 아이고 (놀람 · 감탄)
To be used to show surprise.

dawdle [dɔ́:dl] *vt.* 빈둥거리다, 꾸물거리다; *vi.* (시간을) 부질없이 보내다
To do something or go somewhere very slowly, taking more time than is necessary.

glorious [glɔ́:riəs] *a.* 찬란한, 훌륭한, 영광스러운
Very beautiful or impressive.

adore [ədɔ́:r] *vt.* 숭배하다, 동경하다; …을 매우 좋아하다
To love someone very much, especially in an admiring or respectful way, or to like something very much.

tiddly [tídli] *a.* 거나하게 취한; 아주 작은
Extremely small.

whoop [hu(:)p] *v.* 고함지르다; *n.* 야호 하는 외침, 함성
To give a loud, excited shout, especially to show your enjoyment of or agreement with something.

snatch [snætʃ] *v.* 와락 붙잡다, 잡아채다
To seize or grab suddenly.

tonic [tánik] *n.* 강장제, 활기를 돋우는 것; *a.* 튼튼하게 하는, 원기를 돋우는
Something that makes you feel stronger or happier.

bannister [bǽnəstər] (= banister) *n.* (계단의) 난간
The row of poles at the side of stairs and the wooden or metal bar on top of them.

Build your Vocabulary

MJ ★ **rhinoceros** [rainásərəs] *n.* 코뿔소, 무소
A very large thick-skinned animal from Africa or Asia, which has one or two horns on its nose.

☆ **pant** [pænt] *v.* 헐떡거리며 말하다, 헐떡거리다, 숨차다
To breathe quickly and loudly through your mouth, usually because you have been doing something very energetic.

24. Veruca in th Nut Room

☆ **squirrel** [skwə́:rəl] *n.* 다람쥐; *vt.* 저장하다, 축적하다, 숨기다
A small furry animal with a long furry tail which climbs trees and feeds on nuts and seeds.

복습 **jeepers** [dʒíːpərz] *int.* (미) 이런, 저런, 굉장하군 (놀람·열광의 표시)
An expression of surprise.

J **stool** [stu:l] *n.* 걸상
A seat without any support for the back or arms.

☆ **mound** [maund] *n.* 산더미처럼 쌓은 것 (a mound of tire : 타이어 더미)
A large pile of earth, stones etc. like a small hill.

J ☆ **hollow** [hálou] *v.* 속이 비다[게 하다]; 도려내다, …을 파내어 만들다
Having a hole or empty space inside.

chute [ʃu:t] *n.* 활송로, 자동 활송 장치; 비탈진 수로, 활강 사면로
A narrow, steep slope down which objects can slide.

복습 **knuckle** [nʌ́kəl] *n.* 손가락 관절[마디]; *v.* 손가락 마디로 치다
One of the joints in the hand where your fingers bend.

복습 **cock** [kák] *v.* 위로 치올리다, (귀·꽁지를) 쫑긋 세우다
To move a part of your body upwards or in a particular direction.

복습 **intent** [intént] *a.* 집중된, 열심인 (intently *ad.* 열심히, 골똘하게, 여념 없이)
Giving all your attention to something.

parakeet [pǽrəkìːt] *n.* (작은) 잉꼬
A small parrot with a long tail.

canary [kənέəri] *n.* 카나리아
A small yellow bird which is well known for its singing, and is sometimes kept as a pet in a cage.

soothing [súːðiŋ] *a.* 달래는, 위로하는, 누그러뜨리는, 진정하는
Making you feel calm.

beady [bíːdi] *a.* 구슬 같은
Small and bright, especially like a bird's eyes.

pin [pin] *n.* 핀, 못바늘; 전핀; 장식 핀, 브로치
To make someone unable to move by putting a lot of weight on them.

anchor [ǽŋkər] *v.* 단단히 묶어 두다, 고정시키다; (배를) 닻으로 고정시키다
To make something or someone stay in one position by fastening them firmly.

wretched [rétʃid] *a.* 비참한, 불쌍한; 초라한; 야비한, 비열한
Unhappy, unpleasant or of low quality.

flap [flæp] *v.* 펄럭이게 하다, 퍼덕이다; *n.* 펄럭임, 퍼덕거림; 혼란, 소동
To wave something, especially wings when or as if flying.

furnace [fə́ːrnis] *n.* 노(爐); 아궁이, 화덕
A furnace is a container or enclosed space in which a very hot fire is made.

sizzle [sízəl] *v.* (튀김이나 고기 구울 때) 지글거리다, 지글지글 소리가 나게 굽다
To make a sound like food cooking in hot fat.

frump [frʌmp] *n.* 추레하고 심술궂은 여자
A woman who wears old-fashioned and unattractive clothes.

crisp [krisp] *n.* (보통 pl.) (영) 얇게 썬 감자 프라이, 포테이토 칩
A very thin, often round piece of fried potato, sold especially in plastic bags.

cross [krɔ́ːs] *a.* 기분이 언짢은, 성 잘 내는; 교차한, 가로지른
Annoyed or angry.

nudge [nʌdʒ] *n.* (주의를 끌기 위해) 팔꿈치로 슬쩍 찌르기; *vt.* 슬쩍 찌르다
To push something or someone gently, especially to push someone with your elbow (= the middle part of your arm where it bends) to attract their attention.

topple [tápl] *vi.* 넘어지다, 쓰러지다
To (cause to) lose balance and fall down.

Build your Vocabulary

- **screech** [skri:tʃ] *vi.* 새된 소리를 내다, 비명을 지르다; *n.* 날카로운 소리, 비명
  To make a unpleasant loud high noise.

- **gracious** [gréiʃəs] *a.* 상냥한, 정중한
  Behaving in a pleasant, polite, calm way.

- **brute** [bru:t] *n.* 짐승, 야만인; *a.* 잔인한, 야만적인, 무정한
  A rough and sometimes violent man.

- **drain** [drein] *n.* 배수관, 하수구; *v.* 배수[배출]하다; 다 써버리다
  If you drain something, you remove the liquid from it, usually by pouring it away or allowing it to flow away, and if something drains, liquid flows away or out of it

  halibut [hǽləbət] *n.* [어류] 북방 해양 산의 큰 넙치, 핼리벗
  A big, flat sea fish which can be eaten.

- **rind** [ráind] *n.* 껍질, 외면, 외견; *vt.* 껍질을 벗기다, 껍데기를 벗기다
  The hard outer layer or covering of particular fruits and foods.

  rancid [rǽnsid] *a.* 고약한 냄새가 나는; 불쾌한, (맛이) 고약한
  Tasting or smelling unpleasant because not fresh.

- **lard** [lɑ:rd] *n.* 돼지기름
  A white substance made from pig fat and used in cooking.

- **oyster** [ɔ́istər] *n.* 굴, 조개류
  A large flat sea creature that lives in a shell, some types of which can be eaten either raw or cooked, and other types of which produce pearls.

  liverwurst [lívərwə̀:rst] *n.* 간소시지(liver sausage)
  A type of cooked sausage which contains liver and is usually eaten cold on bread.

  reeky [ri:ki] *a.* 연기가 나는, 그은; 김이 나는; 냄새가 고약한
  To have a strong unpleasant smell.

- **horrid** [hɔ́:rid] *a.* 무시무시한; 매우 불쾌한, 지겨운
  Unpleasant or unkind.

- **astray** [əstréi] *ad., a.* 길을 잃어, 잘못된 길에 빠져, 정도에서 벗어나
  Away from the correct path or correct way of doing something.

dreadful [drédfəl] *a.* 무서운, 두려운, 무시무시한
Very bad, of very low quality, or shocking and very sad.

pander [pǽndər] *v.* (…의 못된 짓 따위를) 영합하다; *n.* 뚜쟁이, 포주, 중개자
To do or provide exactly what a person or group wants, especially when it is not acceptable, reasonable or approved of, usually in order to get some personal advantage.

brat [bræt] *n.* (경멸적) 선머슴, 개구쟁이
A child, especially one who behaves badly.

★ **culprit** [kʌ́lprit] *n.* 죄인, 범죄자
Someone who has done something wrong.

25. The Great Glass Elevator

row [rou] *n.* 열, 줄; 좌석 줄
A line of things, people, animals, etc. arranged next to each other.

slantways [slǽntwèiz] *ad., a.* 비스듬히, 기울게, 기운
To lean in a diagonal position.

declare [diklɛ́ər] *v.* 선언하다, 공표하다
To announce something clearly, firmly, publicly or officially.

alongside [əlɔ́ːŋsàid] *ad., prep.* …에 옆으로 대고
Beside, or together with.

★ **luminous** [lúːmənəs] *a.* 빛을 내는, 빛나는
Producing or reflecting bright light.

lolly [láli] *n.* 단 과자, 엿
A wrapped sweet for sucking or chewing.

jujube [dʒúːdʒuːb] *n.* 대추 젤리; 대추나무, 대추

★ **wriggle** [rígəl] *v.* 꿈틀거리다, 몸부림치다; *n.* 몸부림침, 꿈틀거림
To twist your body, or move part of your body, with small, quick movements.

fizzy [fizi] *a.* 쉬잇 하고 거품이 이는, 청량감이 드는
Having a lot of bubbles; You can use it when something is strangely good, with a bubbling sensation.

Build your Vocabulary

clang [klæŋ] *n.* 쨍그렁, 땡그렁 (소리); *v.* 땡그렁 울리다
A loud ringing sound.

sting [stiŋ] (stung–stung) *vt.* 찌르다, 쏘다; *n.* 찌르기, 쏘기, (동물의) 침, 고통
If something stings you, a sharp part of is pushed into your skin so that you feel a sharp pain.

wasp [wɑ́sp] *n.* 장수말벌; 성질 잘 내는 사람

stagger [stǽɡər] *vi.* 비틀거리다[게 하다]; 흔들리다[게 하다]
To walk or move with a lack of balance as if you are going to fall.

swerve [swəːrv] *v.* 벗어나다, 빗나가다; *n.* 벗어남, 빗나감
To change direction, especially suddenly.

gallant [ɡǽlənt] *a.* (여성에게) 친절[정중]한; 용감한, 씩씩한
Polite and kind towards women, especially when in public.

strap [stræp] *n.* 가죽 끈, 혁대; *vt.* 끈으로 매다, 가죽 끈으로 때리다
A narrow piece of leather or other strong material used for fastening something or giving support.

precipice [présəpis] *n.* 절벽, 벼랑; 위기
A very steep side of a cliff or a mountain.

pat [pæt] *v.* 가볍게 두드리다
To touch someone or something gently.

comforting [kʌ́mfərtiŋ] *a.* 기분을 돋우는, 격려하는; 위안이 되는
Making you feel less sad or anxious.

cling [kliŋ] *vi.* 달라붙다, 매달리다
If you cling to someone or something, you hold onto them tightly.

glimpse [ɡlimps] *n.* 흘끗 보임, 일견
If you get a glimpse of something, you see them very briefly and not very well.

spout [spaut] *v.* 내뿜다, 분출하다; *n.* 주둥이, 물 꼭지
To flow or send out liquid or flames quickly and with force, in a straight line.

ooze [uːz] *v.* 스며 나오다, 새어나오다 (oozy *a.* 스며 나오는, 새는)
To flow slowly out of something through a small opening, or to slowly produce a thick sticky liquid.

M **craggy** [krǽgi] *a.* 바위가 많은, 울퉁불퉁하고 험한
Having many crags.

MJ **hunk** [hʌŋk] *n.* 두꺼운 조각, 큰 덩어리
A large thick piece, especially of food.

J **hurtle** [hə́:rtl] *vi.* 돌진하다, 고속으로 움직이다; 충돌하다
To move very fast, especially in what seems a dangerous way.

mackerel [mǽkərəl] *n.* 고등어 (북 대서양산)
An edible sea fish which has a strong taste.

★ **collision** [kəlíʒən] *n.* 충돌, 격돌
An accident that happens when two vehicles hit each other with force.

tamper [tǽmpər] *v.* 쓸데없는 참견하다, 손대다, 함부로 만지다
To touch or make changes to something which you should not, usually without enough knowledge of how it works or when you are trying to damage it.

Crossword Puzzle

Use the clues and the words in the box to complete the crossword puzzle.

peculiar	fizzy	hollow	cling	spellbound	fling	soothing
spit	naughty	ooze	intent	swell	pat	obstinate
horrid	snatch	adore	repulsive	perch	hunk	comforting
utter	whoop	declare	topple	scuttle	mumble	

Chapter 21-25

Across

1. Unusual and strange, sometimes in an unpleasant way.
3. To take something or pull it away quickly.
4. Extremely unpleasant or unacceptable.
6. Having a hole or empty space inside.
12. When children are _____, they behave badly or are not obedient.
14. If you _____ to someone or something, you hold onto them tightly.
15. Giving all your attention to something.
16. Unpleasant or unkind.
18. A large thick piece, especially of food.
20. Making you feel less sad or anxious.
23. To touch someone or something gently.
24. To sit on or near the edge of something.
25. Unreasonably determined, especially to act in a particular way and not to change at all, despite argument or persuasion.
26. To flow slowly out of something through a small opening, or to slowly produce a thick sticky liquid.

Down

2. To love someone very much, especially in an admiring or respectful way, or to like something very much.
3. To become larger and rounder than usual.
5. Making you feel calm.
7. Having a lot of bubbles; You can use it when something is strangely good, with a bubbling sensation.
8. Having your attention completely held by something, so that you cannot think about anything else.
9. To throw something somewhere using a lot of force.
10. To give a loud, excited shout, especially to show your enjoyment of or agreement with something.
11. To force out the contents of the mouth, especially saliva.
13. Complete or extreme.
17. To announce something clearly, firmly, publicly or officially.
19. To move quickly, with small short steps, especially in order to escape.
21. To (cause to) lose balance and fall down.
22. To speak unclearly and quietly so that the words are difficult to understand.

Comprehension Quiz

1. Which one is not a sign of danger in the Television chocolate room?

A. The Oompa-Loompas move slowly and carefully

B. The Oompa-Loompas are wearing red space suits

C. The Oompa-Loompas work silently

D. The Oompa-Loompas are near the camera

2. What is wrong with the way Mike Teavee talks?

A. He talks too much

B. He mumbles

C. He speaks nasty words

D. He speaks fast

Chapter 26 **The Television-Chocolate Room**

3. Put the stages of television transmission in order.

(- - -)

A. The picture is broken into millions of tiny pieces

B. The pieces are put together like a jigsaw puzzle

C. The pieces whiz overhead to your TV

D. The camera takes a picture

4. When you send the bar chocolate by television, why is it as big as a mattress?

A. Because big is always better than small

B. Because it comes out much smaller than the real thing

C. There is not any reason

D. Because that is the best size for sending chocoloate by television

5. Why doesn't Mike Teavee pick up the chocolate bar from the TV?

A. He doesn't want to eat it

B. He doesn't believe that the Television Chocolate bar is real

C. He doesn't know how to pick up the television chocolate bar from the TV

D. He is waiting Mr. Wonka's permission

Comprehension Quiz

1. When Mike is in a million pieces, what does Mr. Wonka say to Mr. and Mrs. Teavee?

A. Your son will be fine

B. There is no need to worry

C. Only half of him may appear on the TV

D. He is going down the chute

2. Why is Mr. Wonka trying to scare Mike's parents?

A. So they will prevent Mike from eating too much fast food

B. So they will prevent Mike from watching too much television

C. So they will encourage Mike to study about the chocolate factory

D. So they will try to make Mike an chocolate expert

Chapter 27 **Mike Teavee is Sent by Television**

3. Mr. Wonka said that Mike is unharmed, but what do his parents think? (two answers)

A. He will be stepped on at school

B. He will not be able to do anything

C. He should watch more TV

D. They should send him by television again

4. Mike is not more an inch tall. How will Mr. Wonka fix the boy? (two answers)

A. Have him play basketball

B. Put him in the gum stretching machine

C. Feed him a lot of chocolate

D. Give him some vitamins

5. What do these vitamins do?

A. vitamin H • • a. It makes your toes grow as long as your finger

B. vitamin Wonka • • b. It makes you grow horns on top of your head

Comprehension Quiz

1. What is the name of the button on the elevator?

A. Up and Down

B. Up and Out

C. In and Out

D. The Four Sides

2. Why didn't Mr. Wonka push the button before?

(A)_____

3. What did not the village look like?

A. A picture postcard

B. Covered with snow

C. Busy streets full of people

D. Small houses

Chapter 28 **Only Charlie Left**

Comprehension Quiz

1. What happened to Augustus Gloop?(two answers)

A. He is thin as a straw

B. He was squeezed in the pipe

C. He is still fat

D. He is hungry

2. Violet has been de-juiced but she still has a problem. What is it?

(A)_____

Chapter 29 **The Other Children Go Home**

3. What is wrong with the Salt family?
(A)_____

4. What does Mike Teevee look like?
(A)_____

5. What does Mr. Wonka think of Mike Teevee?(two answers)
A. He was stretched too much

B. He is too thin

C. He will be a popular basketball player

D. He will eat a lot of chocolate and get bigger

Comprehension Quiz

1. Why did Mr. Wonka give the chocolate factory to Charlie?

A. Charlie would run the factory the way that he wanted

B. Mr. Wonka want to help Charlie's family

C. Charlie would sell more chocolate and earn more money

D. Charlie would sell all of the secrets to Slugworth

2. Who does Mr. Wonka invite to the factory with Charlie?

(A)_____

3. How does Mr. Wonka move the family?

A. The family move themselves

B. Mr. Wonka moves them with his own limousine

C. By loading them in the glass elevator

D. The family moves from their house by taxi

4. Why don't the grandparents want to go?

(A)_____

Chapter 30 **Charlie's Chocolate Factory**

Build your Vocabulary

26. The Television-Chocolate Room

- **dazzle** [dǽzəl] *vt.* 눈부시게 하다; 현혹시키다, 감탄시키다, 압도하다
  If you are dazzled by someone or something, you think they are extremely good and exciting.

- **screw up** *phrasal v.* 망치다, 결딴내다
  To make a mistake, or to spoil something.

- **speck** [spek] *n.* 작은 반점, 얼룩; 작은 조각, 단편; 적은 양, 소량
  A very small mark, piece or amount.

- **cluster** [klʌ́stər] *v.* 집중 발생하다; 밀집하다[시키다]; 떼 짓다[짓게 하다]
  If people cluster together, they gather together in a small group.

- **knob** [náb] *n.* 손잡이, 쥐는 곳; 혹, 마디; (깃대 따위의) 둥근 장식
  A round handle, or a small round device for controlling a machine or electrical equipment.

- **scarlet** [skɑ́ːrlit] *n.* 주홍색, 진홍색; *a.* 주홍[진홍]색의
  Bright red.

- **dose** [dous] *n.* (약의) 1회분, 복용량; (쓴) 약; 약간의 경험
  An amount or experience of something bad or unpleasant.

- **jiggle** [dʒígəl] *v.* 가볍게 흔들다, 가볍게 당기다
  To move from side to side or up and down with quick short movements, or to make something do this.

- **goggle** [gágl] *v.* (눈알이) 희번덕거리다; 눈알을 굴리다
  To look with the eyes wide open because you are surprised.

- **presto** [préstou] *int.* 얏, 자 보세요 (마술사가 외치는 소리); *a.* 급한, 재빠른, 신속한
  To be said when something appears or happens so quickly or easily that it seems to be magic.

- **march** [mɑːrtʃ] *v.* 행진하다; 진군하다[시키다]; *n.* 행진, 행군
  To walk with regular steps keeping the body stiff, usually in a formal group of people who are all walking in the same way.

- **dash** [dæʃ] *v.* 내던지다; 돌진하다, 충돌하다
  To go somewhere quickly.

Chapter 26-30

- **flicker** [flíkər] *v.* (빛 등이) 깜박이다, 명멸하다
  To shine with an unsteady light that goes on and off quickly.

- **miraculous** [mirǽkjələs] *a.* 기적적인, 초자연적인; 놀랄 만한
  Very effective or surprising or difficult to believe.

27. Mike Teavee Is Sent by Television

- **saint** [séint] *v.* 성인으로 하다, 시성하다; *n.* 성인
  A person who has received an official honour from the Christian, especially the Roman Catholic, Church for having lived in a good and holy way.

- **scatter** [skǽtər] *v.* 흩뿌리다, 뿔뿔이 흩어지다
  To depart or send off in different directions.

- **glare** [glɛər] *v.* 번쩍번쩍 빛나다, 노려보다; *n.* 섬광
  If you glare at someone, you look at them with an angry expression on your face.

- **wail** [weil] *n.* 울부짖음, 비탄, 통곡; *vi.* 울부짖다
  High-pitched mournful or complaining cry.

- **brow** [brau] *n.* 이마; (pl.) 눈썹
  The forehead.

- **flicker** [flíkər] *v.* (빛 등이) 깜박이다, 명멸하다
  To shine with an unsteady light that goes on and off quickly.

- **wavy** [wéivi] *a.* 파도치는, 물결이 이는, 굽이치는
  Having a series of curves.

- **midget** [mídʒit] *n.* 난쟁이, 꼬마; 초소형의 것; *a.* 보통보다 작은, 극소형의
  A very small person.

- **squeak** [skwi:k] *v.* (쥐 등이) 찍찍 울다, 삐걱거리다; 새된 소리로 말하다
  To make a short very high cry or sound.

- **fro** [frou] *ad.* 저쪽으로 (to and fro : 이리저리)
  In one direction and then in the opposite direction, a repeated number of times.

- **palm** [pɑ:m] *n.* 손바닥; 손 안에 감추다 ; 슬쩍 훔치다[줍다]
  The inside part of your hand from your wrist to the base of your fingers.

Build your Vocabulary

* **pistol** [pístl] *n.* 권총, 피스톨
  A small gun which is held in and fired from one hand.

* **shrink** [ʃriŋk] (shrunk–shrunk) *v.* 오그라들다, 줄다; 축소시키다, 움츠리게 하다
  To become smaller, or to make something smaller.

* **tread** [tred] (trod–trodden) *v.* 걷다, 밟다, 지나가다
  To put your foot on something or to press something down with your foot.

M ★ **squash** [skwáʃ] *v.* 짓누르다, 으깨다
  To press something into a flatter shape, often breaking it.

tantrum [tǽntrəm] *n.* 언짢은 기분, 짜증, 불끈하기, 울화
  A sudden period of uncontrolled childish anger.

wee [wi:] *a.* 작은, 조그마한; *n.* 아주 조금, 잠깐
  Small; little.

tricky [tríki] *a.* 교묘한, 까다로운
  If you describe a task or problem as tricky, you mean that it is difficult to do or deal with.

springy [spríŋi] *a.* 탄력이 있는
  Returning quickly to the usual shape, after being pulled, pushed, crushed, etc.

★ **elastic** [ilǽstik] *a.* 탄력 있는, 신축성이 있는
  Something that is elastic is able to stretch easily and then return to its original shape.

★ **foggy** [fɔ́:gi] *a.* 안개가 자욱한; 침침한, 흐린; (생각 등이) 몽롱한; 막연한
  With fog.

overdose [óuvərdòus]
  n. (약의) 과량 복용, 과잉 투여; *vt.* …에게 과도하게 투약하다; 과잉 투여하다
  Too much of a drug taken or given at one time, either intentionally or by accident

* **rare** [rɛər] *a.* 드문, 진귀한
  Not common; very unusual.

idiotic [ìdiátik] *a.* 백치의, 천치의
  Stupid.

loll [lɑ́l] *v.* 하는 일 없이 빈둥거리다; 축 늘어져 기대다[늘어뜨리다]
  To lie, sit or hang down in a relaxed informal or uncontrolled way.

slop [sláp] *v.* 엎질러지다, 엎질러서 더럽히다; *n.* 엎지름, 흙탕물, 진창
To cause a liquid to flow over the edge of a container through lack of care or rough movements.

★ **lounge** [láundʒ] *v.* 빈둥거리다, 어슬렁어슬렁 걷다
If you lounge somewhere, you sit or lie there in a relaxed or lazy way.

hypnotis[z]e [hípnətàiz] *v.* …에게 최면 걸다, 매혹하다, 무력화하다
To put someone in a state of hypnosis.

MJ ★ **ghastly** [gǽstli] *a.* 무시무시한, 송장[유령] 같은, (구어) 지독한
Unpleasant and shocking.

tot [tát] *n.* 어린아이, 꼬마
A young child.

✽ **rot** [rát] *v.* 썩이다[썩다], 못쓰게 만들다; *n.* 썩음, 부패
To decay.

clog [klág] *v.* 막히다, 방해하다
To become blocked or filled so that movement or activity is difficult.

clutter [klʌ́tər] *v.* 어수선하게 하다, 혼란케 하다; *n.* 난장판, 혼란, 소란
A state of untidiness.

✽ **rust** [rʌ́st] *n.* (금속의) 녹; *v.* 녹슬다[게 하다], 부식하다[시키다]
A reddish brown substance that forms on the surface of iron and steel as a result of decay caused by reacting with air and water.

galore [gəlɔ́ːr] *a.* 풍부한
In great amounts or numbers.

★ **wondrous** [wʌ́ndrəs] *a.* (시·문어) 놀랄 만한, 불가사의한
Extremely and surprisingly good or strange.

★ **gypsy** [dʒípsi] *n.* 집시
A member of a race of people originally from northern India who typically used to travel from place to place, and now live especially in Europe and North America.

복습 **smuggle** [smʌ́gəl] *v.* 밀수입하다, 몰래 들여오다
To take things or people to or from a place secretly and often illegally.

Build your Vocabulary

- **isle** [ail] *n.* (시어) 작은 섬; *v.* 작은 섬으로 만들다, 격리시키다; 작은 섬에 살다
  An island.

- **muffle** [mʌ́fəl] *vt.* (따뜻하게 하거나 감추기 위해) 싸다; 약하게 하다[어둡게]
  To make a sound quieter and less clear.

- **oar** [ɔːr] *n.* 노
  A long pole with a wide, flat end that you use to move a boat through water.

- **pirate** [páiərət] *n.* 해적, 해적선, 약탈자; *v.* 약탈하다
  A person who sails in a ship and attacks other ships in order to steal from them.

- **penelope** [pənéləpi] *n.* 그리스 신화에 나오는 Odysseus 아내, 여자 이름

- **rotter** [rátər] *n.* (영·속어) 건달; 쓸모없는 사람, 무용지물
  Someone who is very unpleasant or does very unpleasant things.

- **hump** [hʌmp] *n.* 낙타의 혹
  A round raised part on a person's or animal's back.

- **rump** [rʌmp] *n.* 궁둥이
  A person's bottom.

- **nauseate** [nɔ́ːzièit] *v.* 구역질나다[게 하다]; 혐오감을 느끼다[게 하다], 싫어하다
  To cause someone to feel as if they are going to vomit.

- **repulsive** [ripʌ́lsiv] *a.* 되쫓아버리는, 박차는; 쌀쌀한; 싫은, 불쾌한
  Extremely unpleasant or unacceptable.

28. Only Charlie Left

- **dart** [dɑːrt] *v.* 날아가다, 돌진하다; 쏘다, 던지다; *n.* 던지는 (화)살, 다트
  To move quickly or suddenly.

- **swing** [swiŋ] (swang–swung) *v.* 빙그르르 돌리다, 회전하다
  To move easily and without interruption backwards and forwards or from one side to the other.

- **furious** [fjúəriəs] *a.* 성난, 격노한; 맹렬한, 왕성한 (furiously *ad.* 맹렬하게)
  Extremely angry; Using a lot of effort or strength.

Chapter 26-30

- ★ **hunch** [hʌntʃ] *n.* 군살, 혹; (구어) 예감, 육감; *vt.* (등을) 둥글게 구부리다
  An idea which is based on feeling and for which there is no proof.

- **dilly-dally** [dílidæ̀li] *vi.* (구어) 꾸물거리다, 빈둥대다
  (본문에서는 'dilly'와 'dally'를 나눠서 씀)

- ★ **fetch** [fetʃ] *vt.* (가서) 가져오다, 데려오다, 불러오다
  To go to another place to get something or someone and bring them back.

- 복습 **crane** [krein] *v.* (목을) 쑥 내밀다; 달아 올리다
  If you crane your neck, you stretch your neck in a particular direction in order to see something better.

- **wham** [hwæm] *n.* 쾅(소리); 강한 타격, 충격 *v.* 후려갈기다, 쾅 치다
  To be used to suggest the sound of a sudden hit.

- 복습 **whistle** [hwísəl] *n.* 휘파람, 호각; *vi.* 휘파람 불다, 휘파람으로 부르다
  If something whistles somewhere, it moves there, making a loud, high sound.

- ★ **long** [lɔ(:)ŋ] *vi.* 애타게 바라다; 열망[갈망]하다
  To want something very much.

- M ★ **tempt** [tempt] *vt.* 유혹하다, 부추기다
  Something that tempts you attracts you and makes you want it.

- MJ 복습 **tremendous** [triméndəs] *a.* 거대한, 대단한; 엄청난, 무서운
  Very great in amount or level, or extremely good.

- J ★ **splinter** [splíntər] *v.* 쪼개지다, 찢어지다; *n.* 부서진 조각; *a.* 분리한
  A small sharp broken piece of wood, glass, plastic or similar material.

- J ★ **hover** [hʌ́vər] *v.* 하늘을 떠다니다, 비상하다
  To stay in one place in the air.

- J **eerie** [íəri] *a.* 섬뜩한, 무시무시한, 기분 나쁜, 기괴한
  Strange in a frightening and mysterious way.

29. The Other Children Go Home

- J ★ **hover** [hʌ́vər] *v.* 하늘을 떠다니다, 비상하다
  To stay in one place in the air.

Build your Vocabulary

truckload [trʌ́klòud] *n.* 트럭 한 대분의 짐
The amount of something that can be carried by a truck.

✸ **brim** [brim] *v.* 가장자리까지[넘칠 정도로] 차다; *n.* 가장자리
To become full of something.

복습 **peer** [piər] *vi.* 자세히 보다, 응시하다
If you peer at something, you look at it very hard.

overstretch [òuvərstrétʃ] *vt.* 너무 잡아 늘이다, 너무 펼치다
If you overstretch something or someone or if they overstretch, you force them to do something they are not really capable of, and they may be harmed as a result.

✸ **dreadful** [drédfəl] *a.* 무서운, 두려운, 무시무시한
Very bad, of very low quality, or shocking and very sad.

30. Charlie's Chocolate Factory

♩ ✸ **hover** [hʌ́vər] *v.* 하늘을 떠다니다, 비상하다
To stay in one place in the air.

복습 **cock** [kάk] *v.* 위로 치올리다, (귀·꽁지)를 쫑긋 세우다
To move a part of your body upwards or in a particular direction.

✸ **deadly** [dédli] *ad.* 몹시; 지독하게; *a.* 치명적인; 활기 없는; 따분한
Completely.

✸ **sake** [seik] *n.* 위함, 이익, 목적 (for the sake of ⋯, for ⋯'s sake : ⋯을 위하여)

복습 **mind (you)** *idiom* 알겠니, 잘 들어 둬 (양보 또는 조건 제시에 따르는 삽입 문구)

♩ 복습 **stammer** [stǽmər] *v.* 말을 더듬다, 더듬으며 말하다
If you stammer, you speak with difficulty, hesitating and repeating words or sounds.

복습 **fetch** [fetʃ] *vt.* (가서) 가져오다, 데려오다, 불러오다
To go to another place to get something or someone and bring them back.

✸ **cottage** [kάtidʒ] *n.* 오두막집, 시골집
A small house, usually in the countryside.

✸ **despair** [dispέər] *n.* 절망; *vi.* 절망하다
The feeling that everything is wrong and that nothing will improve.

Chapter 26-30

‡ ruin [rúːin] *v.* 파괴하다, 파멸시키다
To ruin something means to severely harm, damage, or spoil it.

petrify [pètrəfài] *v.* 돌이 되게 하다, 돌같이 굳게 하다, 깜짝 놀라게 하다
To frighten someone greatly, especially so that they are unable to move or speak.

Crossword Puzzle

Use the clues and the words in the box to complete the crossword puzzle.

cluster	hover	palm	dally	slop	dazzle	wail	splinter
stammer	rare	fetch	brim	muffle	speck	flicker	squash
loll	march	glare	scatter	tricky	cottage	dose	tantrum
tempt	shrink	lounge	tremendous				

Chapter 26-30

Across

1 If people _____ together, they gather together in a small group.
3 The inside part of your hand from your wrist to the base of your fingers.
5 To cause a liquid to flow over the edge of a container through lack of care or rough movements.
6 If you are _____d by someone or something, you think they are extremely good and exciting.
7 To look at someone with an angry expression on your face.
8 An amount or experience of something bad or unpleasant.
9 To become smaller, or to make something smaller.
13 To become full of something.
15 A small house, usually in the countryside.
18 To shine with an unsteady light that goes on and off quickly.
19 To speak with difficulty, hesitating and repeating words or sounds.
20 To depart or send off in different directions.
22 To lie, sit or hang down in a relaxed informal or uncontrolled way.
24 To walk with regular steps keeping the body stiff, usually in a formal group of people who are all walking in the same way.
25 To press something into a flatter shape, often breaking it.
26 A sudden period of uncontrolled childish anger.

Down

2 Very great in amount or level, or extremely good.
4 To go to another place to get something or someone and bring them back.
5 A small sharp broken piece of wood, glass, plastic or similar material.
10 Not common; very unusual.
11 To stay in one place in the air.
12 To waste time or do something slowly.
14 To make a sound quieter and less clear.
16 If you describe a task or problem as tricky, you mean that it is difficult to do or deal with.
17 High-pitched mournful or complaining cry.
19 A very small mark, piece or amount.
21 Something that tempts you attracts you and makes you want it.
23 To sit or lie somewhere in a relaxed or lazy way.

Comprehension Quiz Answers

Ch 1   1. C   2. D   3. A   4. B   5. B   6. C   7. C

Ch 2   1. A   2. C   3. B   4. D   5. A-2, B-1, C-4, D-3

Ch 3   1. B   2. C   3. Because it will melt in the hot sun   4. A   5. D

Ch 4   1. B   2. D   3. B   4. C   5. B

Ch 5   1. A, D   2. A-a, B-b   3. D   4. A

Ch 6   1. A, D   2. Eating   3. A, C
          4. (A) famous gangster (B) Charlotte Russe (C) Professor Foulbody   5. C   6. A, C

Ch 7   1. Wonka's Whipple-Scrumptious Fudgemallow Delight   2. B   3. C   4. A   5. D

Ch 8   1. B   2. D   3. He watches too much TV   4. C   5. D

Ch 9   1. C   2. B   3. C   4. A

Ch 10   1. A, C   2. Mr. Bucket lost his job   3. A   4. A   5. C, D
          6. He found a dollar bill   7. A, B

Ch 11   1. A   2. D   3. D   4. C

Ch 12   1. E-B-D-A-C   2. C   3. B   4. C   5. A

Ch 13   (No questions)

Ch 14   1. D   2. B   3. A, B   4. D   5. B, C

Ch 15   1. Enough to fill all of the bathtubs and swimming pools in the country
          2. C   3. Staggered, dumfounded, bewildered, dazzled
          4. A soft minty sugar that looks like grass   5. B, D

Ch 16 1. C 2. D 3. B
4. He smuggled them to the factory in packing cases with holes in them 5. A, B

Ch 17 1. B 2. C 3. C 4. A 5. A

Ch 18 1. A 2. C 3. B 4. D 5. C

Ch 19 1. D 2. B 3. C 4. D 5. B

Ch 20 1. C 2. B 3. A 4. B

Ch 21 1. C 2. C 3. D 4. A, C 5. B

Ch 22 1. D 2. C, D 3. A 4. B 5. A

Ch 23 1. B 2. D 3. A 4. Drunk 5. A, C

Ch 24 1. Only squirrels 2. To see if they are bad nuts 3. D 4. C 5. B

Ch 25 1. Sideways, longways, slantways, and any other way you can think of
2. D 3. Answers will vary 4. D 5. C

Ch 26 1. D 2. A 3. D-A-C-B 4. B 5. B

Ch 27 1. C 2. B 3. A, B 4. B, D 5. A-b, B-a

Ch 28 1. B 2. Because he could not bear the thought of make a great big hole in the roof of the factory 3. C

Ch 29 1. A, B 2. Her face is still purple 3. They are covered with garbage
4. He is about ten feet tall and thin as a wire 5. A, C

Ch 30 1. A 2. Charlie's whole family 3. C 4. They have been in the same bed in the same house for more than 20 years, so they are afraid to move

Crossword Puzzle Answers(Ch 1-5)

Across

3 doze
4 huddle
7 awful
12 extraordinary
13 glisten
14 nibble
15 absurd
16 marvellous

Down

1 torture
2 delicate
3 draft
5 desperate
6 mutter
8 colossal
9 shrivel
10 munch
11 tremendous
13 gobble

Crossword Puzzle Answers (Ch 6-10)

Across

5 bulge
7 fling
8 shrug
9 beastly
11 repulsive
13 tip
14 beckon
15 vague
16 leap
18 cram
19 spoil
20 crane

Down

1 crouch
2 trudge
3 wedge
4 precious
6 hooligan
7 flabby
8 splutter
9 beam
10 luscious
11 ridiculous
12 peer
17 roast
18 clutch

Crossword Puzzle Answers (Ch 11-15)

Across

4 corridor
6 track
9 sheer
11 trouser
14 pupil
17 blissful
19 cock
21 stagger
22 perish
23 seize
24 flap

Down

1 peculiar
2 tremendous
3 verdict
5 dazzle
7 astonish
8 bony
10 envious
12 scrub
13 glimpse
15 twinkle
16 cluster
18 mischief
20 leap

Crossword Puzzle Answers (Ch 16-20)

Across

1. wretched
3. chant
5. grind
6. simmer
8. gorge
12. grin
13. meddle
15. hollow
16. lick
17. grudge
18. dribble
19. feast
20. scramble
22. revolt
23. sneak
24. whiz

Down

2. crave
4. groan
5. gleam
7. inconceivable
9. lid
10. peer
11. shriek
14. dangle
19. fabulous
21. luscious

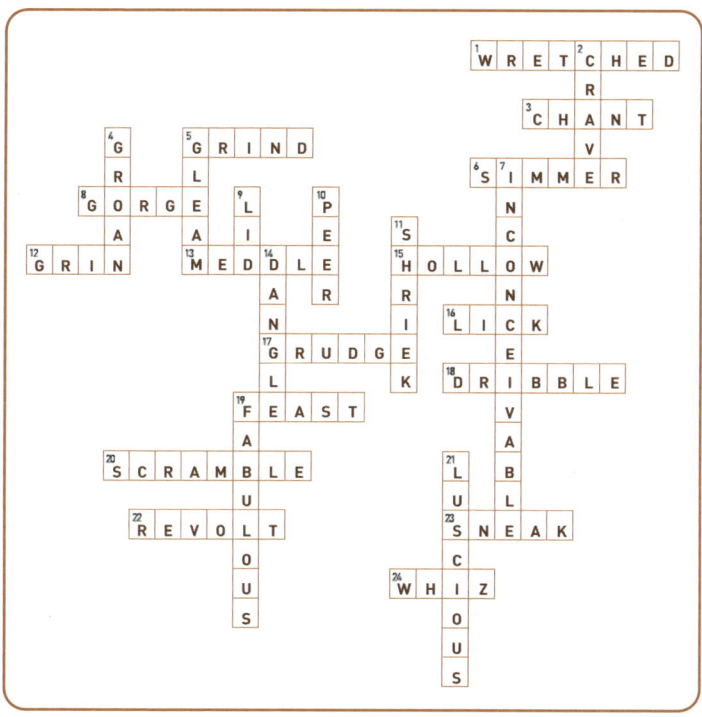

Crossword Puzzle Answers (Ch 21-25)

Across

1. peculiar
3. snatch
4. repulsive
6. hollow
12. naughty
14. cling
15. intent
16. horrid
18. hunk
20. comforting
23. pat
24. perch
25. obstinate
26. ooze

Down

2. adore
3. swell
5. soothing
7. fizzy
8. spellbound
9. fling
10. whoop
11. spit
13. utter
17. declare
19. scuttle
21. topple
22. mumble

Crossword Puzzle Answers (Ch 26-30)

Across

1 cluster
3 palm
5 slop
6 dazzle
7 glare
8 dose
9 shrink
13 brim
15 cottage
18 flicker
19 stammer
20 scatter
22 loll
24 march
25 squash
26 tantrum

Down

2 tremendous
4 fetch
5 splinter
10 rare
11 hover
12 dally
14 muffle
16 tricky
17 wail
19 speck
21 tempt
23 lounge

Charlie and the Chocolate Factory를 완독하셨군요! 축하합니다!

로알드 달의 다른 책도 꾸준히 읽어보세요.

Charlie and the Chocolate Factory를 재미있게 읽으셨다면 Roald Dahl의 다른 대표작인 Matilda와 James and the Giant Peach도 함께 읽어보세요. 같은 저자의 시리즈를 읽다보면 비슷한 문체와 어휘를 반복해서 만나게 되고, 이는 리딩 속도 향상과 어휘력 신장으로 자연스레 이어집니다. Matilda와 James and the Giant Peach의 『원서 읽는 단어장』도 출간되었습니다. 인터넷 서점에서 '원서 읽는 단어장'을 검색해보세요.

무료 단어장을 받아보세요!

다른 원서를 읽을 때도 정리된 단어장이 있다면 정말 좋겠지요? www.readingtc.com/voca를 방문해보세요. 원서별로 어려운 어휘를 정리한 단어장 무료 PDF를 제공하고 있습니다.

모든 원서들의 단어장을 제공하고 있진 못하지만, 비교적 많이 읽히는 원서를 중심으로 꾸준히 업데이트 되고 있습니다. 새로운 원서를 읽기 전에 단어장이 준비되어 있지는 않은가 꼭 한번 확인해보세요!

함께 모여 원서 읽는 〈스피드 리딩 카페〉

어떤 원서를 읽을지 고민이신가요? 원서를 꾸준히 읽고 싶은데 잘 안 되시나요? 그럴 때는 함께 모여 원서를 읽는 〈스피드 리딩 카페 cafe.naver.com/readingtc〉를 방문해보세요. 수준별 추천 원서 목록, 함께 만든 원서별 단어장, 매월 진행되는 북클럽 등 원서 읽기에 도움이 되는 자료가 넘쳐납니다. 무엇보다 원서를 함께 읽을 동료들을 만날 수 있는 멋진 곳이랍니다! 이미 수천 명이 함께 모여 원서를 읽고 있지요. 원서 읽기에 관심이 있으시다면 이곳을 방문해서 함께 참여해보세요!